ADBASHING

Surviving the Attacks on Advertising

Why the Future of Advertising and Media
Depend Upon the Changes
We Make and the Risks We Take Today

American Media Council
of the Worldwide Marketing Leadership Panel

OTHER BOOKS BY JACK MYERS

In Search of Value:
Behind the Scenes in the War for the Consumer's Mind

Cable Television Advertising
State of the Industry 1990-2000

Magazine Publishing
Actionable Strategies for Improving Magazine Performance

For Jan, Andy, Ariele and Danny

With thanks to Sandy Adirondack, Mark Braff, David Derr,
Phil Harding, Gert Myers, Leah Reznick, Donna Schwarz,
Maryann Teller, Tami Clinton,
and Renee Rewiski

Special thanks to
Bob Bolte, Doug Greenlaw, Arnie Semsky, David Houle
and to the "Fast Lane"

With great appreciation to my friends and colleagues
in the advertising and media business who have generously
shared their time and wisdom in support of my efforts

In Memory of David Myers

AMERICAN MEDIA COUNCIL
Worldwide Marketing Leadership Panel

Parsippany, New Jersey 07054
800.551.6937

COVER DESIGN BY
RON CARUSO AND JIM PETRUCCI

COVER PHOTOGRAPH BY
WILLIAM COSTELLO

MANUFACTURED IN THE UNITED STATES OF AMERICA

ISBN 0-9635864-0-8

Library of Congress Catalog Card #93-70442

CONTENTS

PART 5

PART 6

PART 7

PART 1

FACING REALITY:
ARE ADVERTISING AND MEDIA
DYING?

CHANGE OR DIE!

Business is dead. They killed that proposal. It's a dying brand. The Fall 1991 issue of *Best of Business* headlines "Madison Avenue is at a *Dead* End." In business, death and dying is a constant theme. The threat of failure -- of dying -- hangs over every presentation... every business decision. Fear pervades the business community, so much so that any degree of risk becomes unacceptable.

Change, by its very nature, involves risk. So, naturally, business has become change-averse. On the surface the advertising industry appears to be a business where change comes with the territory. Witness the growth of cable television and the upheaval caused by recent governmental regulations. Study the dramatic fragmentation of the magazine industry. The success of *USA Today* has changed the newspaper medium. Changes in the retailing industry and the resulting rise of trade and consumer promotion have come at the expense of traditional advertising. Ad agencies are continually opening and shuttering their doors; agency firings and hirings are taking place at an accelerated pace.

But the state of constant change is deceiving. In reality, the marketing, advertising and media businesses are staid and relatively unchanging. Practices and influences from as far back as the late-1800s are still dictating decisions. In the new media and marketing environment of the 21st century, many of these practices no longer will be relevant.

Worse, these practices are *killing* the advertising business. Adherence to the past and reliance on traditional means of conducting business have precipitated a collapse of the foundation, structures and principles upon which the advertising industry, and our nation's economic support system, are based.

During the past 20 years America's marketing muscle, upon which it built its worldwide economic and political strength, has been sapped. Case studies charting the decline of U.S. industry fill the bookstores. It is time to take a hard look at our approaches to marketing. First, are the resources with which we make marketing decisions relevant to today's corporations? Second, are advertising agencies prepared to respond to the radically altered environment in which they are operating? And third, can media companies react to the explosion of technological advances, the expanding universe of media opportunities and the impact of interactivity?

This book is about change: why and how the marketing, advertising and media businesses must completely change the concepts, premises and strategies upon which they operate. Much of this book is focused on changes that have taken place in society and the hidden impact they are having on the foundation of financial and consumer support for the television programs we watch, the magazines and newspapers we read, the radio stations to which we listen, the products we buy, the stores and locations in which we shop.

It offers a guide for renewing the role of advertising in American life and for recapturing America's marketing leadership. Those in the marketing, advertising and media industries may find this book to be a map for the future or they may be threatened by it. Perhaps both. Those with a more casual interest in the topic should, at the very least, be entertained and, hopefully, be educated about the important contribution marketing, advertising and media make to our everyday lives.

I hope all readers will be enlightened and will think about how they are responding to the reality of a changing world. My goal in writing *ADBASHING* is that all of us in advertising and media may change and thrive and never be forced to confront the prospect of working in a dying business.

PART 2

ADVERTISING UNDER SIEGE:
THE ROLE OF MARKETING,
ADVERTISING AND MEDIA
IN AMERICAN LIFE

ADVERTISING UNDER ATTACK

Advertising is an industry under siege.

Of all the trends having an impact on business today, none is more potentially devastating to the American culture, economy or worldwide influence than the attacks being leveled upon advertising. Advertising, once considered a glamorous career, has sunk in perception among graduating college students to an all time low. Eastern Europe and Eurasia are embracing the concepts of capitalism and its foundation -- media advertising. In the United States, however, a socialized view of advertising and media appears to be gaining momentum. Government and citizens increasingly support a regulatory environment that is restrictive and anti-competitive, as witnessed by the overwhelming Congressional passage of a major cable regulation act camouflaged to appear as a pro-consumer effort.

Rather than celebrating the consumerist culture of America upon which our worldwide political success has been built, many in America are seeking to dismantle it.

The Center for the Study of Commercialism, an organization formed to fight commercialism, blames advertising for everything from homelessness to Americans' predisposition against taxation. One of the Center's published reports, *Dictating Content: How Advertising Pressures Corrupt a Free Press,* suggests that a truly free press requires the limitation or elimination of advertising. Just the opposite is true. The alternatives to ad support are government funding (and control) or totally reader/viewer paid distribution which would result in a dramatic reduction of choice.

"There are some types of advertising we might ban and others we would seek to attenuate by making them more costly," says Michael Jacobson of the Center. "The best way to do that is through the tax laws." The frightening reality is that Jacobson's position is being increasingly supported by federal and state political leaders who consider advertising to be a potential taxation bonanza that would be virtually invisible to consumers while actually costing billions in increased product costs.

Legislators conveniently ignore First Amendment freedoms to censor advertising that they consider to be potentially dangerous. We generally consider bans on cigarette and alcoholic beverage advertising to be in the public interest. Extended bans on beer and wine advertising and print advertising bans on tobacco products are inevitable in the '90s. The Alcohol Beverage Advertising Act, sponsored by a bipartisan coalition of eight Senators, requires health warnings in broadcast commercials, print advertisements and promotional displays for beer, wine and liquor.

The Washington, D.C. "watchdog" group, Public Citizen, holds pharmaceutical advertising targeted toward doctors responsible for the doctors' knowledge and usage of various drugs. The activist group has aggressively supported strict new legislation that would require pharmaceutical companies to submit all ads to an independent review board for approval or lose their tax deduction for advertising. To further its efforts, Public Citizen released data from a UCLA study against the wishes of its author, who admitted: "I'm not sure our data is big enough to say anything...." Yet, based on questionable data from a questionable study, Congress is pressured into taking restrictive, anti-advertising actions. The *Integrity in Prescription Drug*

Advertising Act would create a panel of medical experts, consumers, editors and drug company executives to examine and rule upon prescription ads before they appear. Is this public responsibility or irresponsible attempts to establish precedent for censoring business?

Already, pharmaceutical manufacturers comply with extensive advertising regulations imposed by the U.S. Food & Drug Administration. It is clearly necessary for *any* industry to monitor the accuracy and claims of its advertising, but standards and policies exist to accomplish this end. Further efforts serve the activist groups more than the public they propose to aid. Their own self-interests are served by selling memberships, contributions and magazine subscriptions.

Adbusters, the quarterly publication of the Vancouver-based Media Foundation, regularly lambastes the advertising industry and specific advertisers. One recent parody of Absolut Vodka advertising is headlined *Absolut Nonsense*, and lampoons the real advertising: "Any suggestion that our advertising campaign has contributed to alcoholism, drunk driving or wife and child beating is absolute nonsense. No one pays attention to advertising." The Media Foundation seeks to act as a forum for consumers who object to excess commercialism.

Publications like *Adbusters* and *Utne Reader* and groups like the Media Foundation, which seem to portray advertising and commercialism as a subversive, dangerous form of communications, do little to contribute to society in any meaningful, positive way. The cause of alcoholism is not advertising. Prohibition proved that governmental controls cannot cure a society's problems. Alcoholism was the leading social ill in Communist Russia, where there was total media control and no advertising.

When it comes to attacks on media and advertising, so-called public service groups are frequently self-serving groups seeking only their own aggrandizement by attacking an easy target. Once successful, they move on to other targets. The next "drug" that may well come under their watchful eye is caffeine, followed by aerosol sprays, and then perhaps all non-biodegradable products. Once special interest activist consumer groups gain a foothold, victory in one area only spurs them on to new fights. Once they win one battle, their organization and clout grows, expanding their efforts to dictate America's freedom of choice.

One of the more visible efforts to control media and advertising content has been the *American Family Association* of Reverend Donald Wildmon. Wildmon has sought to use his evangelical base to organize boycotts against companies such as Procter & Gamble and Clorox. Wildmon was never successful in generating any significant public support for his efforts, but has been a master in creating extensive self-promotion and press coverage. Advertising industry trade publications have been particularly generous in covering his actions, especially his attempts in the mid-1980s to organize a grass roots effort to take over CBS. Wildmon's most recent boycott efforts were targeted to "Americans who are tired of having their values ridiculed by Murphy Brown," who were asked to boycott "Murphy" sponsors such as PepsiCo and Bristol-Myers Squibb.

Most Americans ignore such calls to action; many others are offended. A small minority may agree in theory but take no action against the boycott's targets. A minuscule group are vocal advocates of the boycott and forge a broad awareness of their efforts, seeking to impose their will over the broader cross-section of Americans, ultimately acting against the public will and public good.

Only a small minority of Americans realize, according to studies, that advertising is responsible for funding their primary sources of news, information and entertainment. As far back as 1963, David Ogilvy wrote in *Confessions of an Advertising Man*:

"I fear that the majority of thoughtful men will come to agree with Toynbee that 'the destiny of our Western civilization turns on the issue of our struggle with all that Madison Avenue stands for.' I have a vested interest in the survival of Madison Avenue, and I doubt whether it can survive without drastic reform.

"Hill & Knowlton report that the vast majority of thought-leaders now believe that advertising promotes values that are too materialistic. The danger to my bread-and-butter arises out of the fact that what thought-leaders think today, the majority of voters are likely to think tomorrow."

Thirty years after Ogilvy's warning, more than 70% of Americans believe that advertising is a nuisance, up from only 35% as recently as 1960. The impact of these attitudinal changes has not been lost on advertisers. This statistic is eerily reflective of the erosion of budgets away from advertising and into sales promotion and direct marketing. In 1975, advertising captured 65% - 70% of total marketing communications budgets. Today, according to the Association of National Advertisers, the share has shrunk to 25% among packaged goods manufacturers. *Myers Reports* projects that this decline will continue, reducing advertising's share to 15% - 17% by the end of this decade unless dramatic changes occur in the structure, role and perceived value of advertising.

The beneficiaries of advertising's loss have been couponing, direct mail, in-store promotional activities and most prominently, retail trade allowances. These are the direct payments to retailers in return for allocations of shelf space, promotional support and price incentives. Americans find little fault with coupons, promotions, sweepstakes and direct mail that deliver little, if any, social benefit. Why is advertising, which funds a wealth of public services, news, entertainment, events and information attacked as, at worst, subversive and, at best a nuisance?

What is dangerous for the advertising industry and the media community which it supports is the lack of coordinated industry response to these issues. Advertising is as much under attack from within as it is from external influences.

In the late 1800s, Philadelphia retailer John Wanamaker commented that he guessed only half of his advertising worked, but the problem was that he didn't know which half.

That anecdotal comment has become a common refrain among advertisers, but little has been accomplished in 100 years to solve Wanamaker's complaint. In fact, marketers today, who spend $130 billion dollars annually promoting their products and services, are not even certain that as much as half their advertising works. And they are a long way from having pure knowledge of what sells and what doesn't.

Advertising agency BBDO Worldwide recently published a report on brand differentiation. Titled *FOCUS: A World of Brand Parity,* the report states:

"The appropriate question is not whether we believe all consumers are alike but, rather, whether consumers believe that marketers, and more specifically, their products are alike. The unfortunate answer is YES.

It is the knowledge that, once all the research is in, it is only through parity-breaking advertising that we will be able to shatter the worldwide illusion of brand parity."

The clear message is that consumers do not perceive differences between products or between those stores where the products are sold. The equity value of a company -- whether it be a retailer or manufacturer or service company -- depends upon its unique marketing position and the ability of management to maintain and improve upon that position. *Value* lies in the ability of management to differentiate their products and services to consumers through effective marketing communications.

While the American Association of Advertising Agencies (4A's), the Association of National Advertisers and media trade organizations such as the Magazine Publishers of America conduct ongoing efforts to promote the role of advertising, existing efforts are failing to reverse the declining perception of advertising's value to business and to the American way of life.

§

DAVID OGILVY VS. JERRY DELLA FEMINA

In the June 29, 1992 *Advertising Age,* advertising legend Jerry Della Femina wrote about his departure from the agency that bears his name:

"I'll probably start another advertising agency soon. [He has, named Jerry, Inc.] It will be smaller, it'll be happier. Financially, it will be more like Wal-Mart than Macy's. Spiritually, it will be more like 'Hellzapoppin' than the Bank of England. I hope in the next few months to get back in the business I used to be in in the '60s and '70s."

Many in the ad business sympathized with Jerry's desire to return to the good ol' days. But looking to advertising's past as a signpost for the future just won't play anymore. Della Femina's comments had a familiar ring to them. In 1970's *From Those Wonderful Folks Who Gave Us Pearl Harbor*, Della Femina wrote:

"The things that are wrong in advertising would be wrong in any business. But don't get the impression that I don't dig the business. I really do. I could only write about the advertising game this way because I really do love it. Most people say, 'This is a terrible business.' They throw up their hands and go home to Rye at night and forget about it. There are ugly people in advertising, real charlatans, but there are good people, too. And good advertising. And I honestly believe that advertising is the most fun you can have with your clothes on."

In 1970, Della Femina thought advertising was fun. In 1992, he says "The passion is gone, the fun is gone and what remains is cold and serious and quite sad." Announcing the formation of his new agency, Della Femina says "Basically, I want to have fun, and the clients to have fun. That's what's been missing from life." Is the fun missing for Della Femina himself, or is it gone for the whole advertising industry? Advertising *is* a serious business. One of the key paradigm shifts of the 1990s is the reality that the new generation of marketing executives are moving to the top ranks of their corporations.

Their voices are heard in the boardrooms. Advertising has the opportunity to move back up the hierarchical ladder in corporate marketing priorities. Marketers' ability to *measure* results from advertising is a very serious business. In *From Those Wonderful Folks...*, Della Femina writes: "I like to think the work I do is good -- I know damn well it sells the product because my clients wouldn't have anything to do with me if I didn't move the product."

In that one simple statement is the foundation of many of the advertising industry's woes today. Whose responsibility is it to determine if advertising is selling product? Della Femina slightly misstated the reality -- advertisers would have less to do with *advertising* if he didn't move their products. Just when Della Femina published his book, his clients and others began a slow, steady movement of their total budgets out of advertising and into promotional activities.

Della Femina separated himself and his company from the responsibility of determining if, in fact, his work did sell product. The ad industry must heed Della Femina's words, because the reality of how boldly he holds onto the past and challenges those who would present a new, serious vision for the future reflects the great dangers for the industry's future.

The job of the advertising creative, Della Femina implies, is to have fun. Deal with the "cold, serious business" issues elsewhere. Advertising has always been a business that emphasized the creative. There is no doubt that Della Femina's work for clients such as Blue Nun Wine, Isuzu and Purina's Meow Mix has earned him a spot in the Advertising Hall of Fame. But when Della Femina thinks about advertising, it appears he thinks about the creative product alone. In the 1990s, when marketers think advertising, they think sales results first and creativity second.

Advertising is more than the creative output which is visible to the consuming public. Media, research, marketing, account planning and production are an integral part of successful advertising. A constant flow of trade press articles suggests that advertising should return to its roots and concentrate on its primary product: creative. A more cogent vision of the future suggests that the true primary product of advertising agencies is *increased sales of clients' products and services.*

At the 1991 Conference of the Association of National Advertisers, David Ogilvy, founder of Ogilvy & Mather, made a rare appearance to issue a call to arms for the advertising industry. He called for an emphasis on sales results; he decried the industry's need for creative awards. Ogilvy's message can be summed up in words he wrote in 1963 in *Confessions of an Advertising Man.*

"What is a good advertisement? There are three schools of thought. The cynics hold that a good advertisement is an advertisement with a client's OK on it. Another school accepts Raymond Rubicam's definition, 'The best identification of a great advertisement is that its public is not only strongly sold by it, but that the public and the advertising world remember it for a long time as an *admirable piece of work*.'

I have produced my share of advertisements which have been remembered by the advertising world as 'admirable pieces of work,' but I belong to the third school, which holds that a good advertisement is one which sells the product *without drawing attention to itself.* It should rivet the reader's attention on the product. Instead of saying, 'What a clever advertisement,' the reader says, 'I never knew that before. I must try this product."

Ogilvy continued:

"I will not allow [my new employees] to use the word CREATIVE to describe the functions that they are to perform in our agency. The even more fashionable word CREATIVITY is not in the 12-volume Oxford Dictionary....Fairfax Cone would like to blot the word CREATIVITY out of our lives....How did we get along 20 years ago, before 'creativity' entered the lexicon of advertising?"

Throughout his speech to the ANA, Ogilvy emphasized the importance of advertising that <u>sells</u>. But at this conference of marketing executives, Ogilvy was preaching to the converted. Marketers have become progressively more uncertain of the actual return on their advertising expenditures. They question the applicability to their sales of the standard norms of creative effectiveness -- advertising recall and likability testing. Marketing budgets have shifted increasingly from traditional advertising into the more measurable areas of direct marketing, sales promotion and trade allowances, where success is measurable.

Success and growth in the advertising and media businesses depend upon our ability and willingness to embrace new forms of communications. Opportunities abound. They exist in the ways advertising messages are created and where and how they are placed. Advertising is and always should be a creative business.

Creativity extends to every idea that helps sell, build identities for or uniquely position products and services. Creativity exists in new media opportunities, new uses of established media and new ways of communicating marketing messages.

In Section III, I offer several creative and *alternative* media ideas and options. In Section IV, I propose creative ideas for restructuring agency and media organizations and a new vision for research, which is the supportive foundation of our industry.

But first, let me admit that I am a great advocate of traditional advertising in broadcast and cable television, radio, magazines, newspapers, billboards and transit advertising. I've worked in each of these media, including the launch of two publications: *The Syracuse New Times* in 1968 and *Tambourine,* a counter-culture teen magazine in the early 1970s. As important as new and innovative media ideas may be, the truly exciting and meaningful opportunities depend upon greater exploitation of traditional media resources. I believe in advertising; I believe it works. I'm also convinced that we must approach the new millenium with a perspective that sheds traditions and fosters innovation.

A NEW COURSE FOR THE FUTURE OF ADVERTISING

Advertising industry leaders such as Della Femina, Hal Riney, George Lois, Bill Bernbach and others correctly identified breakthrough "creativity" as the advertising industry's primary product for the '70s, and the industry elevated its output to extraordinarily high levels of achievement. The fine distinction between advertising and art was often difficult to detect. Advertising followed the path of Raymond Rubicam's theory that "creative ingenuity" was the primary key to advertising success rather than David Ogilvy's proposition that advertising should sell products and not draw attention to itself.

In the 1990s, the structures, systems and processes by which we conduct business in the media and advertising industries are built upon the precedents established in the era of the "creatives." Ogilvy warned, in 1963, of the penalties that would be paid for an over-indulgence in creativity. In the last 30 years the advertising business has created precedents which are no longer relevant. If we look to the past for direction, we must first gain an accurate vision of the future and regain the capacity to respond to the changes taking place around us.

An inability to respond to change is the most certain path to failure. But before we can change, we must first believe that the future is worth planning and preparing for. We cannot sit back and long for a return to the lost world that Della Femina and his generation mourn.

Dr. Neil Postman, in his excellent book, *Technopoly: The Surrender of Culture to Technology,* points out that the 19th and early 20th century capitalists... Rockefeller, Morse, Edison,

Astor, Ford and Carnegie... had a vision of what the 20th century would be. Their greatest achievement, Postman believes, was not the technologies they created, but their ability to convince their countrymen that the future need have no connection to the past.

I believe that the single most important effort we can undertake in the advertising business is to step outside the box of our past. Change is upon us. The future is challenging us to act; to set a new course for how we organize our businesses, how we create advertising, how we analyze media, how we perceive the role of media and media companies, how we evaluate and measure success, how we go about understanding what the future will bring, and how we react to a vision of that future that is totally unlike anything for which our past has prepared us.

It is time to set a new agenda, built upon new principles and a commitment to reestablish advertising as a marketing *tool for which we all - advertisers, agencies, media and researchers alike - take responsibility. This is an ambitious undertaking, but forces already are moving in this direction. In this book, I will share many of these efforts with you and set forth a new course for the future of advertising.*

THE MORE THINGS CHANGE....

Do you automatically complete the cliche "The more things change..." with "...the more things stay the same?" In business, as in society, we no longer can depend upon stability or consistency. We no longer can expect things to stay the same. Too many businesses today are locked into traditional patterns, cycles and measures of success. These molds must be broken. Paradigms must be changed. Cliches must be discarded.

-- *"Some things never change."*
-- *"Everything old is new again."*
-- *"There's nothing new under the sun."*
-- *"Turn, turn, turn."*
-- *"The past is precedent."*
-- *"All the world's a cycle..."*

We need a new set of paradigms. Our comfortable cliches no longer hold. When we look back, we are held back -- in society and in business. The past no longer provides us with adequate tools for building strategies for the future.

In a recent study, a simple old fashioned clock was shown to a large number of 13 year olds. More than one-third were unable to tell the researcher what time the clock indicated. It wasn't that they couldn't tell time, but they could only tell digital time.

This doesn't represent just a simple shift from one form of time to another. It reflects a way of thinking about life. The generations running government and business today - the generations who are creating advertising and communications - subconsciously think in cyclical terms. The new generation functions in a continuum.

Remember the old fashioned television sets with the dial - channels 2 to 13? Television once offered a limited selection of programs. The announcer could tell us "Don't turn that dial!" with a degree of assurance that we would obey. Like the watch, a TV "dial" is virtually obsolete for a majority of Americans. Television channel switchers are digital, as are our radios and our auto speedometers. The average home has more than 30 channels, with a promise that the number will increase to 60 by the end of this decade. Many homes will have 150 channels! When I was growing up in the 1950s in Utica, New York, TV programming ended for the day after The Late Movie, at 2 AM. We listened to the Star Spangled Banner, saw the jets flying over the Statue of Liberty, and then had only a test pattern to pacify us until 6 or 7 AM, when stations formally signed on. On Saturdays in Utica, there was no TV until 9 AM, when the single local station signed on with Howdy Doody. Television, each day, had a beginning, a middle and an end.

Today TV never ends. One recent morning, I turned the set on at 4 AM and scanned 38 channels with nary a test pattern confronting me.

Society, too, is functioning within a new linear context in which the future is uncharted, new, and not dictated by precepts or perceptions of the past. Life is no longer a cycle; the future is no longer predicated by the past.

THE MORE THINGS CHANGE...
THE MORE THEY CHANGE

In the 1990s, consumers are becoming far more discriminating. Purchases are less conspicuous and far more considered. Society, like the tectonic plates in California, is shifting and resettling into new configurations. Marketers are hoping that the shifts are completed and consumers will settle into a new set of comfortable, somewhat traditional patterns. But more than likely, the shifts are an early warning sign that far more cataclysmic changes are on the horizon. Marketers may be facing shifts in consumer and communications patterns for which there are no precedents and for which they are ill prepared.

In advertising, the nuclear family remains the core of many messages. Yet, census data shows that only 4% - 6% of American homes conform to the traditional family concept of working dad, mom at home and 2.5 kids. In fact, today each child has 2.6 parents! The number of women who are in the work place increases each year. In Minneapolis, fully 75% of that city's female population hold full- or part-time jobs.

GRUBBYS - THE NEW FORCE IN MARKETING

Throughout the 1980s marketers were able to neatly encapsulate the new non-traditional consumer under the "Yuppie" umbrella, conveniently focusing on the "I want it all" me generation. In the 1990s, Yuppies are a rare breed, replaced by what trend forecaster Faith Popcorn describes as *SKIPPYs* (Schoolkids with Income and Purchasing Power) and *WHOOPIES* (Well Heeled Older People). To these acronyms I add the most important new consumer group, *GRUBBYS* - Grown-Up Boomers Struggling to Get By.

Grubbys are distinguished by their lack of preparation for the difficult emotional and financial circumstances in which they find themselves. They were raised on a steady diet of assurances of a better future, and an economy that easily forgave failure. After years of conspicuous consumption, Grubbys suddenly have been put on hold.

The growing importance of the Grubby market also reflects the "middle-aging of America." Demographically, traditional advertising audience measurement services group consumers into convenient age clusters of "under 35," "35-54" and "55+." While these are gross simplifications of consumer characteristics, age and gender are the primary statistics used for media purchase decisions. In the 1990s, the number of total households under 35 years will decline 8% while households 35-54 will grow 30%. households of 55+ will increase 11%. Additionally, the 55-64 year old age group is behaving more similarly today to the 35-54 year old than the 65+ group, suggesting that, for marketing and media purposes, middle age should be considered 35-64.

American Demographics Magazine reports that "Aging will

dominate household demographics in the 1990s. Householders under age 35 will shrink under the weight of an aging baby boom, and the oldest households will grow rapidly during the last half of the decade. But the bulk of household changes will occur among the middle-aged. By decade's end, half of *family* householders will be aged 35-54, compared to 43% in 1990....in 2000, all baby boom householders will be aged 35-54."

The implications of these changes for advertising are enormous. Grubbys no longer are receptive or susceptible to messages based upon "new" or "better" or "a hot product" or "high tech" or "the latest innovation." Today, it's "cost savings," "trial offer," "more for your money," "longer lasting," "better quality," and "greater value." For years, advertising's role was to create and build awareness and brand name retention. Suddenly, pressures have mounted for messages that communicate value and directly motivate consumers to act. Inotherwords, advertising that directly sells products.

This shift in emphasis reverberates across all facets of the advertising industry--from clients to advertising agencies to media companies. The advertising industry today is like a huge factory, still functioning but with antiquated technology: multiple competitors offering identical products result in tremendous commoditization of pricing and declining profitability; aggressive external competition from other industries erodes the revenue base; the work force operates with outmoded strategies; management lacks a clear vision for the future; and the very use and value of the basic product is questioned by primary customers. Jane Cavalier, president of Cox Landey & Partners, contends that the advertising agency business is "choking itself. It's an industry in crisis."

Just as the government has built itself with huge debt, the advertising industry has mortgaged its future as well. Tremendous growth throughout the 1970s and 1980s in overall advertising media expenditures has camouflaged a continual erosion of the perceived value and role of advertising for actually motivating purchase decisions. Marketers increasingly are questioning how traditional advertising media can effectively have an impact on the "Grubbys'" new economic and societal realities. Marketers must seek out non-traditional media opportunities, ask media to do business in new ways and at lower costs, and demand new forms of research focused on sales effectiveness.

THE MARKETING IMPLOSION

During the past 15 years, a dynamic shift in the corporate world has been away from sales and marketing-driven management and toward MBA schooled financial management. Many corporations now are realizing that a balance is necessary and that textbook management, focused solely on quarterly profits, is not productive. Corporations in the 1990s and beyond, are beginning to depend on marketing to maintain and improve their market position and respond to a highly competitive marketplace for which traditional case study training did not prepare financial management. During the next ten years marketing professionals will take over the top positions in their companies as they wrest corporate control from the finance departments.

A 1990 article in *The Marketer,* the publication of the Association of National Advertisers, points out that "Increasingly, consumer goods marketers are being tapped by companies and services that are not marketing-driven and being asked to transform the corporate culture. The reasons why are legion and obvious: all businesses are facing greater competition, increased costs across the board and a consumer body that is about as pesky to define and hit as a mosquito. The marketer -- bless him -- is supposed to divine and manage all of these changes."

What the average marketing manager has experienced, however, says *The Marketer*, "is everything from blank stares at your buzz words to outright hostility at your presence." Throughout the 1990s and beyond, marketing managers will be turned to increasingly for their expertise. Blank stares and hostility will change to desperate pleas for direction.

There are those who believe the bullish economy of the Reagan era was a false economy, buoyed by leveraged buyouts and increased corporate and government debt. These individuals correctly point to low individual savings, decreasing consumer confidence and the sustained economic recession of the early 1990s. While some economists envision a continuing economic slide, I envision an invigorated economy in the second half of the 90s, founded on a return to power of America's marketing management.

Peters' and Waterman's 1980 book *In Search of Excellence* raised the art of Japanese corporate management onto a pedestal. Peters and Waterman identified eight basic practices which they considered to be characteristic of successfully managed companies.

IN SEARCH OF EXCELLENCE
by Thomas J. Peters and Robert H. Waterman Jr.
Harper & Row Publishers, Copyright 1982

EIGHT BASIC PRINCIPLES OF MANAGEMENT:

The eight attributes that emerged to characterize most nearly the distinction of the excellent, innovative companies go as follows:

1. *A bias for action, for getting on with it.*
2. *Close to the customer.*
3. *Autonomy and entrepreneurship.*
4. *Productivity through people.*
5. *Hands on, value-driven.*
6. *Stick to the knitting.*
7. *Simple form, lean staff.*
8. *Simultaneous loose-tight properties. (Both centralized and decentralized.)*

These ideas, they pointed out, represented conventional wisdom in Japanese companies but were not common practice in the majority of American business concerns. Throughout the 1980s, *In Search of Excellence* was a corporate guide, providing management guidance and organizational direction. Yet, the word *marketing* does not appear in the book's summaries of any of these eight basic principles. Nor does the word appear in the book's index. In fact, this treatise on business leadership that set the tone for American corporations in the 1980s, virtually ignores the single most important contributing factor to America's economic might -- marketing.

In the 1990s, corporate organizational experts will focus on executives with marketing and advertising skills. Marketing executives will be elevated by aggressive, forward-thinking companies to senior levels of responsibility and authority for corporate decision-making. These executives will be assured of the support, rather than the "blank stares" or "outright hostility" of their colleagues. Finance executives and investors must be educated about the important role of marketing for generating increased profitability.

When the economy, markets, competition and consumer loyalties were relatively stable, corporations could conduct research and develop strategies with a high degree of confidence that they would be implementing these strategies under the same conditions in which they were created. Positioning opportunities were defined; the keys to competitive advantage were product development, line extension and accurate marketplace positioning.

Today, markets are constantly shifting. A company's competitive advantage is defined by *anticipation* of market trends and competitors' actions, and the speed with which it responds to change. Business success today is less a factor of product quality and more a measure of organizational behavior and identification of customer needs. Increased competition results in fewer qualitative differences among competitors. In an era of relative product parity, the goal is to identify the unique organizational capabilities that distinguish one company from its competitors.

Media companies and advertising agencies sell their services primarily based upon the products they create. Although most advertising executives would describe their businesses as "service" companies, they are, in reality, in the product business: developing a variety of products ranging from television commercials to media plans. Television, radio, magazine and newspaper companies are selling time and space, which they have successfully converted from abstract concepts to well-defined and restrictive parameters.

Throughout the advertising business, company management must rethink their answers to the simple questions: "What is the task? What are we trying to accomplish?" These questions must be asked of every employee, and the answers should be consistent. The average corporate middle manager is likely to respond by identifying tactics, i.e. "reducing overhead," "buying more efficiently," "winning creative awards," etc. Today, in the advertising business there should be only one answer: "We are selling our clients' products and services."

THE NEW RISK-TAKING MANAGER

The focus on short-term tactics is consistent with the demands of financial management for immediate profits, reducing a corporation's willingness and ability to take risks. "Upside potential vs. downside risk" dictates corporate decisions. The acceptable degree of risk has become smaller and smaller in American corporations until almost any risk has become unacceptable. During the next 15 years, corporations will slowly *increase* the allowable risk as it becomes apparent that competitive leadership requires risk. Risk aversion is an indication of fear, and companies in the 1990s require assertive exploration and exploitation of opportunities. Business failures today are caused more by a lack of marketing capabilities and vision than as a result of a poor economy. Those who gain a clear vision of their consumers and their competition, and who are willing to take intelligent risks with sound future-thinking marketing strategies, can succeed even in a poor economy.

Peters and Waterman idealized Japanese management techniques in the early 1980s; their respect was well-placed and American corporations sought to emulate these techniques. But a study of Japanese corporations in America establishes that their marketing departments are run by Americans who are given a powerful voice in management decisions. They are given the resources to succeed and the right to fail.

As we emerge from the recession of the early 1990s, some companies will have failed, others will be failing, and others will be thriving. The difference will not be real estate value, which has been depressed; nor will it be inventory value or effectively

negotiated debt load. Instead, success will have been achieved by
- managements' willingness to accept risk-taking by management;
- the effective evaluation of potential new streams of revenue;
- the ability to manage change;
- the development and maintenance of clearly defined and well-directed consumer marketing communications programs.

Companies that are marketing-driven will be more adept at assessing and managing risk. In a marketing-focused company, risk is measured against long-term profit potential and realistic measures of performance. Performance can be evaluated by a variety of criteria, from sales and market share to proprietary consumer and trade research. In companies that are measured only by quarterly financial statements, risks that detract from short term profits become unacceptable.

In the 1990s, we are witnessing a shift from short-term profit orientation to mid-term performance evaluation. In the past decade, companies that have assessed their activities on a quarterly basis have given new products and advertising campaigns a very short window to succeed. Marketing driven companies will reverse this process as they recognize the time required to have an impact on a sales curve and as they have clearly defined marketing systems to measure performance against goals.

THE REBIRTH OF BRAND LOYALTY

Several studies have tracked the disintegration of brand loyalty during the 1980s. Brand equity, which took years to build, has eroded as corporations have concentrated their marketing efforts on short-term promotional activities and simultaneously cut back on the percentage of their marketing budgets devoted to establishing brand equity.

Companies generated brand loyalty for their products at a time of minimal competition and when mass media were available at comparatively low costs. They aggressively promoted their brand image and identity through mass media advertising.

As consumers became less homogeneous in their tastes and the numbers of products increased, competition became fiercer. Manufacturers shifted strategies away from mass media and toward targeted marketing and promotional couponing efforts, attempting to incent customers to purchase their products. Ultimately, the marketing process has imploded on itself; companies have emphasized price cutting, promotions and trade allowances. The more price cutting and couponing they do, the more consumers expect them and base their buying decisions solely on price. The more trade allowances offered by marketers, the more demands retailers make in return. As marketers have placed more emphasis on short-term gains, their profits have eroded and the long-term equity value of their brands has collapsed. Now companies are faced with the challenge of rebuilding brand loyalty and rebuilding profits at a time of intense competition and fragmented, expensive media.

To respond to this challenge, business requires a new set of paradigms. Whereas corporate marketing executives have been operating under financially restrictive parameters, future corporate directions must *entitle* them to act aggressively and creatively. A complete reversal of the strategic/tactical balance should be considered.

There has been a myth, in corporations, that they operate under the umbrella of long-term strategies. Management-by-objectives, five year plans, 18 month plans... these are the myths created by management to give a semblance of logical structure to their financially motivated decisions. Several books have paid homage to Japanese management's commitment to long-range planning. But even this is changing.

One senior executive of a leading Japanese-owned corporation commented that long-term planning in his company now meant six months. Yes, they still write five, ten and even 20-year plans, but they revise them every six months. In reality, long-term plans are fictitious. The myth has been created that tactical actions are based on long-term strategies. The corporation of the future will reverse this paradigm:

-- they will identify the short-term tactical business opportunities first,
-- focus on how to capitalize on these opportunities,
-- and then build the long-term strategies based upon their ability to maintain an opportunistic approach to their business.

In the past, companies defined strategies and then attempted to identify the immediate tactics that would lead to the success of the strategy. This is putting the cart before the horse. In the 1980s, General Motors' strategy was to become more cost-competitive and profitable by merging the manufacturing and design of its divisions. During this period, it became obvious to GM's corporate marketers that the greatest *tactical* opportunity was to clearly differentiate their product lines and serve various market fragments. Yet the engineering division manufactured products that were clones of each other. Japanese competitors were marketing clearly differentiated and well targeted products. Marketing executives from American auto manufacturers became like the old-fashioned elixir salesmen trying to sell their cure-all products in a modern drug store. Too often in the past, corporate strategies have been determined without the input of marketing trends and marketplace realities.

There's the story of the blacksmith who prided himself on molding the finest horseshoes and having the fastest service. Upon the introduction of the automobile, he set his strategy to produce more horseshoes and speed up his service even more to assure that he could capture the lion's share of the smithing business. He hired more blacksmiths and increased his space. One day, a young auto mechanic walked in and asked for some free space to fix autos. In return, he would give 50% of his business to the blacksmith. But the blacksmith said no, because the loss of space would be counter to his strategy of improving his turn-around time on shoeing horses.

This apocryphal story is indicative of the many counter-productive actions taken by business caused by blind adherence to strategies that are not based upon marketplace realities and are not responsive to tactical marketplace opportunities. More and more, companies in the 1990s will seek to identify the tactical opportunities and build strategies that can take maximum advantage of them. Corporate funding will be available to enable management to act immediately once opportunities are identified.

A major issue for big business in the 1990s is how effectively it can adjust and restructure organizationally to take advantage of new business realities. Most major companies have had significant staff cuts in recent years. Marketing and research departments have been especially hard hit. Brand and product management have focused heavily on their short-term business needs, spending the majority of their time and efforts on distribution and promotional efforts.

Research budgets have been cut, as companies depend upon syndicated quantitative data rather than in-depth proprietary insight into consumer attitudes and dynamics. Corporations may not have adequate systems or personnel in place to gain knowledge of consumer perceptions and define tactical marketing opportunities. We've all witnessed the rapid conversion over the past several years of our local supermarket and mass merchandiser from the traditional cash register to sophisticated scanner equipment. The availability of data from scanners has brought a new level of sophistication to retail sales analysis.

Yet, with all the research and information marketers and media have available to them, their satisfaction with research to assist in their ability to make marketing decisions is declining. Scanners report what has happened. But it doesn't tell them *why*, and it, for now, doesn't tell them *who*. The cost of scanner data is high. It serves the needs of financial management, but not marketing management. The shift in corporate control between these two groups over the next several years brings a commensurate need for improved focus on *who* and *why*, not simply *what*.

WHY HAS AD SPENDING GROWN SO MUCH?

Advertising grew from a $12 billion business in 1963 to $95 billion in 1989 and to an estimated $130 billion in 1992. If marketers question its value for selling products, how was this sustained growth possible? Why have advertising expenditures grown? Primarily because the number of products being advertised has expanded exponentially.

Advertising continues to be the most viable and cost efficient means for getting a product's name and message in front of the most people in a short period. The more products there are, the more important it is to establish product awareness and identity. In 1970, 30 individual models of advertised automobiles were manufactured by four American companies, General Motors, Ford, Chrysler and American Motors. Today, more than 375 individual models from 40 companies compete for attention, trying to break through and create sufficient interest to bring interested buyers into the showroom.

In 1970, the average suburban supermarket stocked approximately 9,000 individual items. Today, the average supermarket stocks more than 22,000 items, including many of its own brand names. In the early 1970s a brand could control a dominant share of market and maintain its share with a reasonable amount of advertising. Prell Shampoo, for example, had a 40% share of market in 1972. Today, Prell's share is less than 3% and its parent company, Procter & Gamble, must spend significantly more on advertising and promotion to maintain that share.

◆

LIVING IN A MEDIA WORLD

We live in a society dominated by media.

Two-thirds of Americans tell researchers that television is their primary source of news and information. Speaking to the California Institute of Technology in 1991, President Bush said: "Ours is an economy increasingly dependent not on our natural resources or geographic location. Ours is an age of microchips and MTV." Television sets our national agenda. Magazines, radio and newspapers confirm and give substance to that agenda.

When Ross Perot appeared on CNN's *Larry King Show* and commented that he would consider running for President if *the people* wanted him to, hundreds of thousands responded, creating a grass roots candidacy. *USA Today*, national magazines and newspapers immediately made Perot their lead story, giving him almost more press visibility than all the Democratic candidates combined during the primary season. When Perot dropped out of contention for the Presidency, his advisors claimed that Perot was simply not willing to conform to the demands of a traditional campaign and would not invest heavily in *traditional* television advertising, as his advisors recommended. Perot's original candidacy and his subsequent re-entry made an important contribution to the political season: the use of the televised "town meeting" to create a sense of community between candidate and the people. Perot's campaign was centered almost entirely around the long-form use of the television medium.

The reality is that television *is* the community of our nation. Perot's television town meeting concept hit a responsive chord because television is now our meeting place, where we identify our social issues, learn our news, meet people we like and gain a sense of perspective on the world around us.

Media also helps us define our issues and causes. Jacques Cousteau has done more for creating awareness of the quality of ocean life than all governmental and public groups combined. Your can of tuna has a little dolphin-safe symbol on it because of a 1963 Chuck Connors movie called *Flipper*, which gave birth to a television show of the same name. The movie continues to be shown constantly on The Disney Channel, Cinemax, and independent stations, without any footnote that before *Flipper* we had no sense that dolphins had real intelligence and real personalities.

We learn about our world and our history from media.

In one week in 1993 on cable television, there were more programs devoted to the history of wars fought by the United States than appeared in one year in 1973. Equally, there arc more programs on nature and the environment. Every *day* the average American home with cable television receives 88.5 hours of news programming; in 1972 the same home received only six hours of news. The available amount of business news has expanded from minutes each day to hours. CNBC offers a steady diet of consumer affairs programs. Religious programming, once relegated to a few Sunday morning hours, now airs 24 hours daily on several different networks.

In the 1960s, only *American Bandstand* offered a daily merger of television with music. Today, MTV, VH-1, Country Music Television and The Box offer around the clock video music.

At 7 AM on one day in August 1992, the average cable home in a large city had a choice of three network and one local talk shows, CNN and Headline News, financial news, eleven cartoons, three exercise programs, three different choices of music programming, news in Japanese, two Spanish programs, one sports news program, coverage of the Congress and Senate, coverage of a major court case, two documentaries, a cooking show, two shopping channels, and four movies.

In 1992, the Time-Warner cable system in Queens, New York became the largest cable system in the country, offering 23 channels on its Broadcast Basic Tier; 32 additional Basic Cable Networks; six local information channels; 11 pay sports and movie channels; two Spanish stations and one each of a Chinese, Greek, Indian, Korean, and Japanese channel; 18 channels in stereo; plus 56 pay-per-view movie channels for virtual viewing-on-demand. Its offerings include two religious channels, five home shopping networks, five educational networks, and extensive local service programming. The cable guide lists nearly two thousand movies each month, plus Comedy Central, Black Entertainment Television, two C-Span networks and Court TV, two public access channels, a channel devoted to NASA news, plus a national sports network and two regional ones.

We are awash in information and entertainment. Today in America, there are more than 22,000 newspapers and periodicals, 500 million radios, 100 million computers and nearly 200 million television sets. There are 27,000 video outlets and nearly 60 billion pieces of junk mail delivered every year.

Just in television alone the changes that new technologies have wrought impact on much more than *what* people view; the affect they have on how and why they view. In 1961 former Federal Communications Commission Chairman Newton Minow complained that television was "a vast wasteland." In the 1960s, Paul Klein of NBC put forth that television viewers sought out the "least objectionable program."

Today, viewers report that they are more actively *seeking* programming that suits their individual needs and interests. The sheer weight of availability of television programming has restructured viewing patterns from the "least objectionable programming" to "most desirable programming." Remote control technology now enables viewers to roam among multiple choices, and viewers report that they often watch two or more programs simultaneously. Fifty percent of all homes have two or three television sets, allowing different household members to view the programs of their own choice.

Marshall McLuhan argued that television "is like the juicy piece of meat carried by the burglar to distract the watchdog of the mind." McLuhan believed we watch TV because of our mood or out of habit, instead of tuning in to see something in particular. Today, viewers are becoming more proactively involved in their viewing selections. The use of a remote control, video tape and interactive television converts the viewing process into an active, rather than passive, process. This reality, the impact of which we have hardly begun to recognize, completely alters the medium as an advertising vehicle. If you think that media and advertising have changed in the past ten - 20 years, just wait until the next ten!

The concept of advertising was radically changed by the advent of the printing press, and has changed relatively little since then. Before the printing press, products were dependent upon the spoken word communicated individual to individual. The elixir salesman was a traveling commercial. The printing press, which spawned the newspaper and magazine, introduced the concept of interspersing editorial with paid announcements - or advertisements. Television and radio borrowed the technique, intercutting commercials with programming. Electronic media extended the capabilities of advertising, but the basic role and relationship of the media and the advertising message today remain unchanged from the early days of print.

In the 1990s and beyond, emerging electronic capabilities will totally and completely alter how the individual receives an advertising message. The traditional print based interrelationship between the editorial content and advertising content, between the medium and the audience, will be restructured. Radio enhanced print by adding sound. Television added sight, sound and motion. The next major capability breakthrough is interactivity.

Just as television added sound and motion to print, new technologies are providing the equally, if not more, important component of interactivity to audiences and, therefore, to advertisers. This represents more than an enhancement. It is a radical alteration of the medium.

CD-ROM, fiber optic, databasing, and Personal Digital Assistance (PDA) technologies will cause virtually all advertisers to develop totally new creative and media strategies focused on personal, detailed, transactional relationships with their audience. This book is a not a forum for describing these new technologies. There are other sources far more detailed than I have set out to provide in this book on how each of these technologies work. Suffice to say that interactivity - personal interactivity - is here and now. It will have an impact upon advertising that represents more of a paradigm shift than the introduction of radio or television. The only event of equal magnitude was the invention of the printing press.

From the time the printing press was invented in the 1700s until the mid-1900s no meaningful technologies were introduced that altered the basic form or context of communications. Western culture had more than 200 years to adjust and adapt to the printed word. Educational systems still in place today were built around the availability of printed books; representative government depended upon freedom of the press. Telegraphy and telephony represented the first major change to this structure, introducing new forms of access to information. Photography, broadcasting and computer technology followed, further advancing the form, volume, speed and substance of communications. Today, interactivity is bringing sweeping change to how people access and use their communications systems. Fiber optic technology is radically advancing the state of communications art.

Imagine television viewers being given the opportunity to simply push a button on their keypad to request immediate transmission of a special introductory coupon for a new food product just advertised. Along with the coupon comes special supplemental coupons from a local retailer, giving an added incentive if the customer comes to their store. Once used, the redeemed specially coded coupon triggers a follow-up special offer delivered into the consumer's electronic mail box requesting, in return, answers to a few marketing questions, which are then transmitted in real time directly into the company's research database.

Or consider a car commercial. Today, the same Chevrolet commercial goes out on *60 Minutes* into all homes nationally.

Some regional distribution is available, but on a limited basis. In just a few years, an advertiser will be able to transmit simultaneously different commercials into different homes, preselected based upon household characteristics. Each household will have the choice of entering personal interests into their interactive reception device, which will automatically decode and deliver the appropriate commercials. The device will store which commercial was delivered, whether or not the television was on, who the primary viewer of the set is, and whether or not the viewer requested specific follow-up information from the advertiser.

Each week, advertisers will receive an electronic printout of actual commercial ratings, along with regional distribution, viewer characteristics and the percentage of viewers who requested an interactive response. Viewers' requests for information will either be immediately printed out on a laser printer built into the television set or fulfilled via fax, mail or home computer.

Is this all blue sky? Does it bring us closer to Big Brother? To both questions, the answer is 'no.' All of the technological capabilities either exist or are now being developed. They increase individual control over media consumption - not reduce it. They have the choice of receiving advertising messages and directly interacting with companies of their choice. New technologies integrate direct marketing and sales promotion techniques into television, reducing message clutter and enabling marketers to control the distribution of their communications to customers who are most receptive to them.

Why do these changes represent radical change rather than simple enhancements? Return with me to the days of yesteryear - to the age of *Donna Reed* and *Ozzie & Harriet*. Come with me into their homes. It's 1959. There's the TV; sure, it's black & white and looks antiquated, but it works the same as today's TV. There's an old fashioned Fridgedaire; the electric lights are on; Ozzie's leaving to go on a trip - driving to the airport. The oven is not a microwave, but it cooks just as well. Ricky's playing an electric guitar and listens to the transistor radio when not talking to a buddy on the phone. We can watch *Ozzie & Harriet* and, other than it being in black & white, we do not experience culture shock. Life was different. Television was different. But in material ways, life on the 1950s and '60s sitcoms closely mirrors life today on *Seinfeld* or *Home Improvement.* (Except, perhaps, that we see more television sets in the 1960s sitcom homes. Today's TV characters, except for *The Simpsons*, rarely watch television.)

Now, let's visit an average American home in 1893. The changes are overwhelming. Pa is leaving on horseback or carriage to travel to a neighboring town and won't be back for days. There's no television or phone. No refrigerator. In material ways, the culture shock from 1893 to 1959 was enormous.

As we look back from 2023 to 1993, will it be a shock? Or will our 1993 surroundings look relatively comfortable and familiar? One thing is certain; the way individuals interact with their communications devices will represent a radical departure from the past. And this is the issue with which today's media and advertising executives must grapple as they prepare for technology's next generation.

$$\begin{array}{c}\bullet\\\diamond\end{array}$$

DAN QUAYLE, MEET MURPHY BROWN AND HOMER SIMPSON

Even without technological advances, we are a society that is becoming more involved with our media. The line between television fact and fiction is often and easily crossed. When sitcom character *Murphy Brown,* played by Candice Bergen, became pregnant in 1992, her TV baby shower was attended by several leading television news anchors, including Katie Couric of the *Today Show*, Paula Zahn and Faith Daniels. This set the stage for the public outcry when Vice President Dan Quayle used the Murphy Brown character as an example of a negative role model for his vision of the American family. Quayle, never having watched *Murphy Brown*, and his speech writers were unprepared for a public who perceived and accepted Murphy as a "real" person. Since reality had already crossed into fiction in the program itself, Quayle's words struck as an attack on a real situation, not simply on a fictional character. It allowed Murphy to incorporate the vice president's actual comments into the 1992 Fall season premiere and for the character to respond, in kind, to the real Quayle. What was fiction and what was reality? For the first time, a fictional television sitcom had a dramatic impact on the nation's political scene.

Print media supported these perceptions. Moving Quayle and Candice Bergen/Murphy Brown to the front pages, *Esquire* created a two page cover headlined "Women We Love...and the dummy we don't. The Dan Quayle Even He Doesn't Know." We should not underestimate, nor should we forget, the role *Murphy Brown* played in the outcome of the Presidential election.

The single parent home has been an accepted fixture on television since the *Andy Griffith Show* (although Aunt Bee was a grandmother-figure) and in *My Three Sons* with Fred MacMurray. Quayle, the heir to newspaper fortunes, and a member of the television generation, should have been more sensitive than most to the power and impact of television. But by attacking Murphy Brown, and then admitting he never watched the program, he became an outsider to a public that feels closer to its television characters than to its elected officials. Quayle has most likely never watched *The Simpsons, In Living Color, Northern Exposure* or *Beverly Hills 90210.*

Of all the programs on television, *The Simpsons* may present the most compelling portrayal of Quayle's traditional, albeit dysfunctional, family life in America. A father struggling to make ends meet. Three children, each with a unique set of personality disorders. And a non-working wife who fights a winning battle to keep her family intact. Like *Murphy Brown, The Simpsons* often crosses the barrier between fiction and reality, bringing real life (true, they're animated, but do we notice?) characters such as Michael Jackson into the story lines and constantly lacing the background animation with social commentary.

In Living Color, Northern Exposure and *90210* all offer viewers a sense of community - groups that different segments within society would love to enter. *Northern Exposure* takes place in the remote town of Cicely, Alaska. How many of us would like to live in a place where we were totally free to be as eccentric or different as we pleased without being judged; where we could be ourselves and be totally accepted whether we were Jewish or Eskimo, astronaut or spiritualist, a 61-year-old bartender or his 24-year-old significant-other, a paranoid chef or his hypochondriac wife.

Beverly Hills 90210 offers a different type of community, but one that is equalling appealing to many. An affluent, fast moving group of teens actually have their heads screwed on right, and, when they don't, they are set straight. Some commentators have suggested that each episode is a one hour morality play, populated with kids our kids would like to know and providing more social direction than many teens are getting at school or in their own family life. These are kids from broken homes... wealthy traditional families... alcoholic homes. Some parents are very successful and others are out-of-work; some of the kids are well-adjusted, some are not. But they are all surviving. Like a fireplace on a cold winter night, they create a cozy environment where audiences can curl up and feel warm for an hour each week.

We never criticize those who admit to "curling up with a good book and getting lost in its pages." A book is written to capture readers, to involve them. How many times do we pick up a book and can't put it down until we're done? It's the same with theatrical movies. They're judged by how absorbed we become in the story; how believable the characters become to us. In my high school days in the 1960s, a half hour before classes each day was devoted to a review of the previous evening's prime time programming. *The Man from U.N.C.L.E., I Spy, The Dick Powell Theater, The Fugitive* captured our imaginations. In the late 1960s, it was *Rowan & Martin's Laugh In.* In the 1970s, *Dallas* launched a wave of prime time soap operas that served to revitalize and re-energize that genre and *All in the Family* totally changed the face of television comedy. In the 1980s, reality dramas such as *Hill St. Blues* brought a new dimension to prime time programming.

Television is often criticized when it is too involving, when it achieves the same level of absorption as books or movies. Yet, year after year, night after night, it does achieve this level. A 1990 survey found that 72% of Americans didn't know their next door neighbor. Television understands that the idea of ties and relationships attracts us. What is *Cheers* if not an enclosed neighborhood "Where everybody knows your name. And they're always glad you came." In a world of strangers, television offers us friendship. A recent study of 21 - 25 year olds commissioned by MTV revealed that their favorite program was *The Brady Bunch*. Nick-at-Nite Network, originally programmed as a nighttime fill-in for Nickelodeon, has emerged as one of cable's most popular and heavily viewed networks. Consisting almost exclusively of off-network sitcoms from the 1960s, Nick ran a promotional campaign naming Dick Van Dyke as Chairman, charged with the task of "Preserving Our Precious Television Heritage." The 1950s, '60s and '70s programs have a universal appeal among all age groups. My eight-year-old son's favorite vintage Nick-at-Nite show is *Get Smart*. Mine too. (We also both watch *Ren & Stimpy* along with my 17-year-old son and 14-year-old daughter.)

Is it that these programs were so good? Some were. Some weren't. What keeps viewers coming back is their familiarity with the programs. The toughest challenge for any new television program or magazine is to attract an audience the first time and then to keep them coming back. Building loyalty takes time. Nick-at-Nite has the advantage of built-in loyalty for all its programs. Many of today's most popular shows subtly co-opt the loyalty factor from other shows. *Knots Landing* is a knock-off of *Dallas*; *Melrose Place* shares characters with *90210*.

Totally Hidden Video has not-so-surprising similarities to

Candid Camera.   Lucille Ball, Dick Van Dyke, Carl Reiner, Norman Lear, Phil Silvers, Jackie Gleason, Danny Thomas, Ozzie & Harriet, Fred MacMurray and Bob Cummings are paid homage day in and day out on prime time television. Even *In Living Color* owes a small debt to Milton Berle and Sid Caesar for its off-color ribaldry and kinetic energy. In an almost perverse analogy, the *Mitch Miller Show* and *Your Hit Parade* with Gisele MacKensie and Snooky Lansen were the MTV of their time.

Whatever technique they use, from familiar story lines to famous stars, media seeks to achieve a level of familiarity that breeds loyalty. Viewer tastes are fickle. Today's hit can be tomorrow's flop, the most visible example being ABC's *Twin Peaks*. Different programs appeal to different people. *Thirtysomething* galvanized a generation that identified with individual characters and tracked their own lives, causes and concerns through the lives of these characters.

When *Thirtysomething* was abruptly cancelled, its fans had their close friends ripped away. Fans of the program compared their reaction to being immersed in a great novel and having it taken away three-quarters of the way through.

Television and advertising executives must come to grips with the issue of viewer involvement. It is the first step on the road to interactivity and represents both a challenge and an opportunity. Viewers require a greater degree of consistency in programming and scheduling. Once created, expectations must be fulfilled.

OUR LOVE AFFAIR WITH MEDIA

We complain about the lack of leisure time, the fast pace of our lives. Yet, most of us in America find time to watch television and to read magazines and newspapers. The average adult spends 40% of his or her free time with media, according to *The Free Time Study* conducted by The University of Maryland. While the amount of free time is declining, the percentage of free time devoted to media is increasing. We have come to view our media choices increasingly as a commitment rather than a disposable commodity.

The greatest asset media offer to advertisers is the *need* that most people have for their regular dose of the familiar. In a world that is constantly changing and, at best, in which the future is uncertain, we are comforted by the newspaper at the doorstep each morning, by the presence of familiar programs, our favorite newscaster and sports announcers, by the familiar formats of magazines and words of favorite writers.

Magazines and newspapers are there when they're expected. Television, though it flows along day in and day out, is a medium of many, many parts. Each program, whether it be a soap opera or newscast, is a separate unit with both loyal fans and transient one-time viewers. While the print media have maintained a clear vision of the relationship they have with their readers, television has never quite understood its relationship with viewers.

Programmers cavalierly have shifted programs from one time and night to another. Programs are cancelled with hardly any notice given. They disappear and suddenly reappear weeks later. Imagine a magazine treating its readers this way. For how long would they remain subscribers or continue to pick up the publication at a newsstand? How can loyalty be built without a fair expectation of it being reciprocated?

Television is a whole composed of hundreds, if not thousands, of parts. Each half hour or hour on each channel is a separate entity in the eyes of its viewers. Networks like MTV introduced a new concept -- the vertical network -- with one consistent program type 24 hours a day.

After several years, it became apparent that viewers simply perceived MTV as having a series of three to five minute segments rather than one continuous program. As a result, MTV and similarly programmed networks like CNN and E! Entertainment Television shifted away from short form programming to more traditional 30 and 60 minute structured programs. Although the average person watches television for 25 - 35 hours each week, they watch programs. They no longer watch the least objectionable program... whatever happens to be on. Instead they subscribe to individual programs as they subscribe to magazines. They view the *most desirable programs*. Networks must sell audiences on sampling a program and, once sampled, convert first-time viewers to regular subscribers. Once making a commitment, viewers expect to have their product available to them as ordered.

When a network and studio own a property like *Thirty-something* which has incredible brand loyalty with a lot of life left in it, it is a disservice to their loyal viewers and a disservice to their shareholders to discard the brand without further development. The reasons given for the cancellation were financial -- the program was simply too expensive to produce primarily because the program's success had driven up the stars' salaries. The problem, though, is not stars' salaries or escalating production costs. The problem is a system that is financially structured based on traditions of the 1960s and 1970s with little relevance to audience or advertiser needs of the 1990s.

CBS is the first of the three major broadcast networks to demonstrate some understanding of this process. Through their innovative marketing whiz, George Schweitzer, CBS introduced the concept of recruiting viewers through traditional marketing techniques. While they didn't approach the sophisticated direct marketing techniques of Time Magazine or Sports Illustrated, they developed sweepstakes, heavily promoted their new season premieres through partnerships with Kmart, Nabisco and others. The effort generated an upsurge in sampling that led to CBS' upset win in the 1992 television season.

CBS-TV also understands the value of viewer loyalty. When NBC cancelled *The Golden Girls* and *In the Heat of the Night* after the 1992 season, CBS immediately picked up options on the programs. Their hope was to provide stronger lead-in programming to attract audiences to other new CBS shows.

CBS' actions speak to either a cold statistical logic or a sensitivity to millions of Americans who spent a happy Saturday night with the *The Golden Girls*. Like the loss of a friend, the cancellation of the program would have hurt, but diminished into a fond memory. To these millions of fans, their friend has been saved. CBS, in addition to gaining ratings, also may gain corporate goodwill and accomplish something many in the industry thought it had lost: its image as the premier broadcast network.

In the Heat of the Night consistently beat NBC's *Seinfeld* as well as Fox's *Melrose Place. Golden Palace* has helped make CBS competitive on Friday nights.

PART 3

❖

WINNING BIG
IN THE NEW
MARKETING, ADVERTISING
AND MEDIA ENVIRONMENT

TRADITIONAL MEDIA AND THE
IMPORTANCE OF FREQUENCY

Many of my opinions about the value and potential of media were formed in my earliest days of media sales. My first industry job, back in 1970, was with Metromedia, in its transit advertising division, selling bus advertising in the New York market. When I graduated in 1969 from Syracuse University with a degree in Radio-Television, my goal for my first job was in the creative or production department of a major ad agency. But 1970 witnessed the first of many economic recessions that interfered with my generation's career goals. A $12,000 salary selling bus advertising looked very appealing after three months of pounding the pavement looking for a job.

Don Robinson, my first sales manager, had a creative mind and new ideas for bus advertising that none of the old-timers would consider taking out to their clients. Robinson's idea was the Basic Bus, where one advertiser would buy all advertising on a given bus: inside, outside or both. Not knowing any better, I took the concept to New York advertisers who had never used the bus as a media "vehicle." I approached companies like WABC Radio, Bowery Bank and *The New Yorker* Magazine.

I quickly learned that advertising agencies require quantitative evidence of cost efficiencies, which I could not provide. All I could offer was intuition, logic and potential. Fortunately, several agencies and clients were willing to accept this. At *The New Yorker*, Hoyt (Pete) Spelman and Dick Lord, of agency Lord, Geller & Federico, lined the inside of buses with *New Yorker* cartoons, for which the magazine was famous, and the first use of the now famous line "Yes, The New Yorker."

At Bowery Bank, the client and its agency, Ogilvy & Mather, developed a series of ads for inside the bus, each ad featuring a response card offering different bank services, turning each bus into a virtual branch bank. The response was overwhelming. And at Grey Advertising, the late Mel Goldberg, who was the managing executive on the Gordon's Gin business and an industry legend, took the concept a step further and purchased the total outside of the bus: front, back, sides and the lighted spectaculars that lined the top of New York City buses in the 1970s.

The lessons learned from Don Robinson have lasted for a career. **One: Repetition is essential to get results. Two: Dominate the medium whenever you can. Three: The agency can help, but the client is the key to selling a new idea. Four: Clients want new ideas, but they also want involvement from the medium on executing the idea.**

The concepts for *The New Yorker*, Bowery Bank, Gordon's and subsequent advertisers resulted from many meetings I held with agency and client executives and the fact that I was willing to get fully involved with them. The support I received from my management and the time I was allowed to progress through the selling process, were essential to my success.

I translated this same knowledge to subsequent jobs at WPLJ (the ABC-FM flagship in New York) and CBS-TV.

In 1973, WPLJ (Port Wine and Lemon Juice) was converting from highly formatted, automated progressive music to one of America's first album-oriented rock and roll stations, with a touch of top 40 influence borrowed from its sister station, WABC-AM. In those days, FM was a step sister in the radio industry. Few cars had FM, and AM stations still dominated the rock scene. WPLJ featured a group of disc jockeys, many of whom have become fixtures in the New York market. But at the time, Jim Kerr, Tony Pigg, Pat St. John, John Zacherle, Jimmy Fink and Carol Miller were all hoping to move the station from 20th in the market into the top 10.

Jim Kerr, WPLJ's morning man, had particularly dismal ratings and was not a favorite of the station's general manager, Willard Lochridge. To his credit, Jim was advertiser-friendly and offered to do personal appearances at retail stores. The question was whether anyone would show up. Under pressure to generate sales, I'd jump at any opportunity. I noticed that Jim had a slight ratings spike among women 18-34 between 7 AM and 8 AM. I guessed that these were young clerical workers getting ready to leave for their jobs. Norman's Leather Hut, at Fifth Avenue and 56th Street in midtown Manhattan, had been responsive to the idea of advertising on WPLJ, but wanted some guarantees.

For a grand total of less than $3,000, I scheduled four Leather Hut spots each morning between 7 AM and 8 AM for two weeks. The spots promoted Leather Hut, but they primarily focused on two personal appearances that Jim Kerr would make at Leather Hut on the final Thursday and Friday of the campaign. On the Wednesday before, Jim hyped the appearances throughout all four hours of his show, at no additional cost to Leather Hut. Norman had seen some business increases during the two weeks, but was very wary, as were Jim and I. We hoped 50 customers would show up. The general manager bet us the number wouldn't surpass 20. As Jim, WPLJ's Sales Manager Larry Divney, and I walked to Leather Hut, we saw police activity and crowds. Jim's appearance had attracted nearly 250 people on day one and an equal number during the second appearance. More importantly, Norman's Leather Hut almost sold out of merchandise.

Find the target audience and dominate them. Get involved. Identify the need and target all efforts toward meeting that need.

I also gained appreciation for the extraordinary value of the relationship between talent and the audience. Jim Kerr is not the best looking individual, but to his listeners he was "gorgeous." Through his power of communications, he commanded his audience to meet him at the Leather Hut, and his presence motivated them to buy. Marketers who use stars as spokespersons are seeking access to that same power. The potential for live commercials on radio and hosted television programs (such as *The Tonight Show*) is enormous. Whether you're a fan of radio personality Howard Stern or believe he is the scourge of the universe, he is among the best salespeople in media today. He understands how to convert his audience appeal into selling power and put it to work for his advertisers. He clearly understands that his talent is most valuable when he is able to use it to satisfy his sponsors. The attacks by the Federal Communications Commission on Stern and Infinity Broadcasting are attacks not only on the First Amendment but also on the foundations of capitalism and on Stern's millions of listeners and hundreds of advertisers.

Another WPLJ story offers a different, but equally compelling lesson about the importance and value of client relationships.

Crazy Eddie is more than a New York retailing legend. He's an indicted criminal and alleged stock fraud conspirator. But in 1975, he was thriving as one of the fastest growing audio-video retailers in the New York area and was an important client for any rock 'n roll radio station. Eddie was WPLJ's (which was now the fifth highest rated station in New York) largest billing client.

Eddie had 'hustle' down to a science. His commercials promised the guaranteed lowest prices in New York. All the customer had to do was "shop around, get the lowest price and Crazy Eddie would beat it." Of course, many customers never bothered to shop around, and accepted the price tags on Crazy Eddie merchandise. Needless to say, Crazy Eddie was a profitable business.

Eddie's sell was a very personal one, and many customers walked in and asked to see Eddie himself. When I walked in for the first time and asked for Eddie, it wasn't until the salesman realized I was selling -- not buying -- that he admitted to *not* being the real Eddie, but his "cousin." Every salesman was Eddie, and every salesman *really* was Eddie's cousin.

After clearing some security checks, I was directed out the back door, down the streets and into an unmarked building. Up some rickety stairs was the real Eddie and his Uncle Eddie, who controlled the checkbook. I became one of the few salesmen in New York radio to venture weekly to Brooklyn to visit Eddie. I got paid promptly by Uncle Eddie, keeping ABC's credit department happy, and would sit with Eddie developing commercial ideas. This was before he was on TV and before his Crazy Eddie character became famous, caricatured on Saturday Night Live. My contribution was the "Christmas in July Sale," which became an annual event.

The bottom line of this story is the bottom line. Eddie had a deal. No rate increases within a contract period, no matter what. He negotiated a price one time and that was the price. As a smart negotiator, Eddie had cut a three year deal just as WPLJ's ratings were beginning to take off. Most stations found negotiating with Eddie so daunting that they simply kept the same rate year-to-year, thankful for the business.

But WPLJ had grown dramatically and, under Larry Divney's and my direction (I became local sales manager in 1976), inventory was virtually sold out. It became essential that Crazy Eddie's rates increase in the middle of his contract. Although we knew this would mean probable cancellation, we had no choice but to approach him and accept the expected loss of his business.

Larry and I still talk about our memorable trip to Brooklyn together. It became one of those moments in a career that you always remember, one that comes back to influence you time and again. Instinct had pulled me back to Brooklyn each week to service my clients. I called Eddie to tell him that Larry, whom he had not met, would be joining me to to discuss a rate increase. When we walked in that day, Eddie asked Uncle Eddie to join us. Larry Divney is one of the all time great sales executives in radio and television history (he's now executive vice president of Comedy Central) and his instincts were working overtime that day.

Eddie turned to him and asked him why he'd come. Larry, to his credit, avoided any mention of a rate increase. Instead he told Eddie that I'd said he was one of the great up and coming retailers in New York and he just wanted to meet him. We talked for about 90 minutes, about everything but a rate increase. We subtly let him know that we'd be forced to "walk" from his business, but we hated to do it. As the meeting ended, Eddie turned to Larry and said "Jack is family. Send a new contract to Uncle Eddie."

It's the first time a client had referred to me as "family." To me, I was doing a job without realizing it was any different than the job every other sales person was doing. In retrospect, to be considered a part of *that* family was not necessarily a code of honor, but I was there every week. I was involved. And the result was that WPLJ got a rate increase and I held onto my largest piece of business, without which I wouldn't have made my annual budget. And Larry Divney became a lifelong supporter and advocate.

Since then, I've been told many times by clients that I'm a "part of their family." It's satisfying; it's really just smart business.

WPLJ also taught me a lesson about selling. Pic-A-Shirt, on Ocean and Avenue I in Brooklyn, was another client I forced myself to call on month-in and month-out. When I visited the store for the first time, the owner asked me if I was the station's new "flavor of the month." I'd just joined the station and been given the "grunt list" -- responsibility for calling on the station's least desirable clients and prospects. Pic-A-Shirt was on that list. Typically, salespeople earned their "stripes" with local retail accounts and then, usually within three months to six months, were assigned to call on the more valuable local advertising agencies. Especially in a major market like New York, agency media buyers control millions of dollars in ad budgets. To make an excellent living, salespeople have only to respond to business that has already been committed to their medium and negotiate for a share of that business.

The retail grunt lists in major markets are considered the training ground, away from which salespeople progress as quickly as possible. When confronted with the "flavor of the month" issue, I challenged Mr. Pic-A-Shirt to wait for six months. If I visited him once a month for six months, I asked him to give me a contract in month six, and then every month for at least six months after that if I continued to visit him monthly. Since salespeople from other stations with which he did business visited him only quarterly, and more typically once annually, he called my bluff. I won. He lived up to his end of the bargain. Three years later, when I left WPLJ to move to CBS Television, Pic-A-Shirt was still a client. I hadn't seen him in about 18 months but called regularly to say hello and to be certain that the new salesman was calling on him regularly.

Continuity and service translated into business. I also learned that advertisers rarely established lasting relationships with media representatives. Instead, on the occasions when a media executive did call on an advertiser, it was often because the station had either lost business or was making a one-time effort to close a sale. The concept of learning an advertiser's business needs and then responding to those needs was not in the average radio or television station's business training book.

I took these concepts and experiences to CBS, where I convinced the sales management of WCBS-TV in New York that the station would benefit from a strong retail selling effort. Headed by Mike DiGennaro, Gail Trell and Sherm Wildman, the station restructured its management organization to experiment with my ideas. Business boomed and the concepts were extended beyond retail to fashion apparel and other business categories.

As in anything, most of my success at CBS was experience, educated risk-taking and effort, but a degree of luck was involved as well. The greatest stroke of luck was that a management team was in place that encouraged and supported risk-taking. There were less fortunate events as well. I'd hired a young salesperson and was encouraging him to do some speculating -- cold calling on clients who did not advertise on television but seemed to be ripe. After one month of effort, he couldn't convert a sale. Worse, he couldn't get past first base -- identifying a prospect and getting the first appointment.

After discussing the problem, I guessed that salesperson was suffering from fear of rejection. Rejection is a reality in selling and should not be feared, but welcomed. It takes several losses in order to get a win. With the salesperson in my office, I picked up the phone and called a new store in New Jersey operating in a location that had just been vacated by Sym's, a successful discount clothier which built its business with TV advertising.

Asking for the owner, I identified myself as calling from CBS Television. Now, granted, the power of CBS takes away a lot of the cold call rejection because I invariably could get through to my target -- once. When the owner came to the phone, I introduced myself and congratulated him on his new store, wishing him luck. CBS, I told him, was particularly interested in tracking his success because an important client of ours, Syms, had been successful in that location. We, therefore, anticipated his success as well, and expected that he might be interested in television advertising at some future time.

Did he expect that might be the case for his business? It was difficult for him, with this obvious play on his ego, to say no. Would he mind if we brought him some information on Sym's success story, and our observations of how Sym's grew their business so successfully? Again, he welcomed the opportunity. My salesperson and I made the sales call, but didn't close the sale, even after three more visits. Unfortunately, one year later, our prospect's business had failed. More importantly, the salesperson has gone on to have an extremely successful career in television network sales and sales management. The luck was that I got through to the owner, got in the door, and still demonstrated that the world -- and a career -- would not end with a rejection.

In addition to the successes and failures I experienced throughout my six years with CBS, I came face to face for the first time with the explicit bigotry expressed toward those who threaten the status quo. Upon being named to the local sales manager's job at WCBS-TV, with only radio sales management as background, I met with hostility from many of those whom I now had to manage. One of these sales executives, Deitz Ginzel, confronted me with absolute consternation that the local sales manager's job was being restructured to focus on retail and new business development, rather than focusing on ad agency sales management.

Dietz, and others like him, forced me to spend an inordinate amount of time dealing with internal politics and fending off assaults. Ironically, Dietz moved on to become International Sales Manager for Turner Broadcasting in the mid 1980s, before his sudden and tragic death in a flying accident. While in that position, he was quoted in a trade press article commenting that media companies should focus on their clients' marketing objectives. Dietz had become a believer.

In corporate politics, taking the risky positions is fraught with danger and constant battle. What continued to be my greatest asset at CBS was the management support I received. I developed systems with which we could demonstrate measureable success for advertisers and built a constituency of clients who relied upon me for continual advice on television advertising.

Many of my earliest retail clients continued to be my strongest allies throughout my years at CBS. When I arrived at CBS, Bloomingdale's, the famous retail fashion chain, had unsuccessfully tried television twice before. A new marketing executive, Arthur Cohen (now executive vice president of Paramount Pictures), was committed to another attempt at making television advertising work. After several meetings, Arthur and I determined that we would experiment with a totally new media approach.

We met with the folks from Grey Advertising who worked on the Bloomingdale's business, and convinced them to hold off on creative development until the media strategy was set. The media campaign would be so radical, we advised them, that the creative would have to be equally unusual. One of Bloomingdale's objections to television had been that the audience reach was too large. Their primary medium, *The New York Times*, reached only 11% of the market.

Based upon this knowledge, I analyzed research which demonstrated that the Late News programs on the three network affiliates (WCBS-TV, WABC-TV and WNBC-TV) reached a combined 35% of the market nightly, and had a demographic profile similar to that of the *Times*. Further, I used the analogy to the full-page and two-page spreads that Bloomingdale's used in the *Times,* and convinced Cohen to lock in multiple spots on each newscast each night for 10 nights in support of a major White Sale event.

I credited the formula to my experience with the Jim Kerr Morning Show at WPLJ. *Find the target audiences and own them.* The difference was creating the logical sales pitch that related to Bloomingdale's traditional newspaper lingo. Ninety commercials aired on three stations in 10 nights exclusively between the half-hour of 11:00 AM to 11:30 PM. It was a radical and unheard-of strategy. Advertisers had mostly used television for reach -- not frequency. Grey Advertising, in the spirit of the experiment, created 13 different commercials, each featuring actress Erin Grey presenting a new idea for "How to Be a Hit in Your Bedroom." Bloomingdale's featured different white goods (towels, linens, etc.) manufacturers in each commercial, collecting vendor support dollars from each. The event was a smash hit, increasing sales by as much as 30% over the previous year's sales. After Cohen left Bloomingdale's, he was replaced by Gordon Cooke (who had witnessed Bloomingdale's success from a competitive vantage point at Macy's). Cooke maintained and built on the successful strategy for nearly 10 years.

The concept was copied by retailers nationwide and in Canada, where the CHUM Group of Stations and the Television Bureau of Advertising adopted many of the formulas we had created at CBS. At CBS, in 1977, we put the basic concepts into a program called F.I.R.S.T. (Framework for Insuring Retail Success with Television).

The concepts, formulas, strategies and principles created in 1977 are particularly salient in the 1990s, when advertisers of all types are increasingly demanding that their advertising perform for them. They are looking to insure success. We became so confident for awhile at CBS that we actually agreed to guarantee sales success for our retail clients if they followed our advice. We got involved in creative and media execution, and established research techniques for measuring results of attitudinal changes.

Saks Fifth Avenue, Robinson's L.A., Venture Stores in St. Louis, Marshall Field's in Chicago, Clover Stores in Philadelphia, B. Altman & Company, Waldbaum's Supermarkets in New York and hundreds of other large and small retailers became loyal followers of the techniques initiated at CBS. When I formed my own company in

1984, Saks Fifth Avenue was among my first clients, as was the CHUM Group of Canada. Although I was employed by CBS, Saks' management had viewed me as "one of their family" and a valued consultant.

Success is really not that difficult to achieve. It requires thinking that transcends traditional media approaches; that elevates media to a position of prominence in the advertiser and agency hierarchy; efforts that place the advertisers' marketing objectives first in developing and executing media plans -- ahead of media cost efficiencies and quantitative audience size measurements.

HOW CAN MEDIA CHANGE?

Cable television, magazines and other more targeted media have the greatest potential to benefit from a new focus on the role of frequency. Marketers historically have accepted the theory that a three times frequency is sufficient for most media campaigns. In 1978, researcher Bruce Eckman and CBS put forth the five time frequency theory: *awareness, recognition, retention, purchase decision and purchase motivation.*

Today, I'm suggesting a *12 time* frequency approach to media. Radical? Overkill? I think not. Homes that had three to six television signals just a few years ago now have up to 75 choices, and that number promises to at least double in the next few years. There are several hundred *major* consumer magazines, well up from under 100 when Herbert Krugman of General Electric first put forth his three frequency theory of media effectiveness.

Consumers today are exposed to in-store media. Try to think of a moment in your life when you are not exposed to some form of commercial message exposure, even if it is only the labels on your clothing or the imbedded logo in a bar of soap.

Ken Auletta, in *Three Blind Mice,* concluded that the average American is exposed to nearly 5,000 commercial messages *daily.* The radical increase in media exposure and the dramatic changes in the consumer marketplace demand radical changes in the levels of frequency necessary to achieve success.

Is it logical, with the many changes that have taken place in media, to think that the three times frequency level will work as well as it did in 1960 or even 1980? I don't believe it is.

I'm convinced that advertisers should lock into specific

audiences and achieve an **effective** frequency level of a minimum of 12 times. What is often missing in frequency analyses is the frequency curve. If the average is three, then a percentage is higher and a percentage is lower. Are a few people seeing the campaign 10 times and many seeing it only once? Or are the vast majority seeing it a full three times?

My suggestion is that the majority of the audience be exposed to a campaign at least 12 times within a relatively short period for it to achieve direct sales results. Of course, the creative execution must ask for the sale as well. For messages intended to achieve only brand awareness, the frequency level can be distributed over a longer period. For a major promotional push, frequency can be concentrated and even elevated beyond 12.

Many readers may be thinking that high frequency will naturally be accompanied by a backlash of overwhelmed viewers and readers. The purpose of advertising *is* to make an impact and a 12 time frequency today is no more effective than a five time frequency was in the 1970s.

I have no research or supportive documentation to prove my 12 frequency theory. Can I, as a researcher, justify this? Yes, because I know it works. I've experienced it.

Frequency is the holy grail of the advertising business. It always has been. We just never paid attention. Research proving these theories will be developed, but I have the utmost confidence that empirical knowledge will be supported by research methodologies designed to measure advertising's ability to achieve defined marketing objectives.

MEDIA BUYING OF THE FUTURE

Media buyers require a new set of rules for media planning and buying directions. As a guidepost for media decisions, the objectives of an advertising campaign must first be clarified: awareness, interest, retention, decision or purchase motivation. If the objectives are to motivate consumers to purchase a product or service, then significantly higher levels of frequency are required than if the purpose is to establish brand name awareness. These decisions have significant impact on the choice of media and the uses of media.

For example, a motivational campaign intended to drive sales for a new product with a limited budget suggests that the media choices should be determined based upon how the advertiser can best achieve an average frequency of 12 times against a well-targeted audience. It is more important for this advertiser to reach one million people 12 times than 12 million people one time each.

The means for accomplishing this type of frequency require a radical rethinking of traditional media buying approaches. Buyers can select key magazines and purchase several pages within a single issue. In the fashion industry, Ralph Lauren and Calvin Klein have successfully implemented this strategy for several years in *The New York Times Magazine* and selected fashion publications. Calvin Klein's dramatic and highly publicized 1992 "outsert" packaged with *Vanity Fair* magazine is the perfect example of how a very limited budget can achieve maximum impact through frequency.

Full sponsorship of special feature issues of magazines offers similar issues. Chris Whittle, chairman of Whittle Communications, has built his media company into a several hundred million dollar business by emphasizing the value of dominance and impact through frequency. Whittle's media properties offer controlled reach to highly targeted audiences with exclusive category presence. Chris Whittle envisions a time when an advertiser might buy one complete night of prime time programming on broadcast and cable networks. Coke recently purchased one spot per hour on all U.S. networks and internationally on CNN and MTV for one night.

CapCities is offering advertisers the opportunity to buy a roadblock on the ABC-TV and Radio Networks, the owned television and radio stations, plus ESPN, A&E and Lifetime, in which CapCities have an interest. Spots will run as near to simultaneously as possible on all the properties. CapCities' intent is good as an expanded reach vehicle, but advertisers are certain to want to buy the roadblock at a discount. An advertiser might be more interested in selecting key ABC Network programming and locking their advertising into that programming week after week. Or buying spots on Lifetime, A&E and ESPN in every other commercial break throughout prime time for one week. Or buying a dominant position on one of the ABC Radio networks for one year. In radio, a major advertiser could literally dominate a radio network or local station for comparatively little money. An upscale marketer might invest just a few million dollars to be the dominant advertiser on every classical radio station in the country.

The keys are to determine an objective, identify those media that best reach the target audiences, and develop strategies to achieve media dominance among those audiences. It may be necessary for advertisers to pay premiums to media for the right to implement these innovative media executions, but advertisers have expressed a willingness to pay for greater impact and effectiveness.

WHAT COMES FIRST, THE APPLE OR THE CART?

As we progressively move, in the 1990s, into the *Era of Frequency Dominance*, marketers will require new forms of research and demand increased emphasis on the performance of media in achieving specific objectives. Advertisers and agencies will put media ahead of creative decisions. Once a choice of media type has been made, there is typically little contact between media and creative departments. Media buyers may never see the creative execution until the advertising actually appears, and creative executives rarely see a detailed media plan.

What comes first in advertising, the media plan or the creative execution? Some think the two are separate and distinct, a combination of metaphors. Creative and media are the horse and the cart, the apple and the tree. They go together. They are not the horse and the tree.

Because frequency decisions have a critical impact on the creative execution, the shifts toward increased frequency will force the marriage of the two. Media ideas will come from the creative team as well as the media department. For example, a decision to run a magazine insert vs. multiple pages in a single publication vs. single pages in several publications requires totally different creative executions. Advertisers who run several commercials during a single television program, as Bloomingdales's did, require multiple versions of a campaign theme.

The role of the Knowledge Resources Manager becomes critical to the implementation of successful media campaigns. The Knowledge Resources Manager pulls together agency and client resources and assures that they match up with the goals of the campaign.

Media, however, must be willing to escape from the traditional confines of their sales structures. When WCBS-TV launched the Bloomingdale's campaign, the computerized traffic program had to be rewritten. A traditional guideline for advertisers and agencies is that a commercial for the same product should not run within 20 minutes of itself. In a 30-minute program, the maximum number of commercials that the same advertiser would run is typically two. The computer control system at WCBS-TV was written accordingly, automatically rejecting schedules placing an advertiser's commercials too close to each other. Bloomingdale's required three commercials within the half hour; before the station would allow the rules to be changed -- rules that had been in response to advertisers' demands -- it took several days of discussion and debate among station management.

Media tend to become locked into traditional ways of doing business. The concept of selling premium positions in television is considered heretical, even though newspapers and magazines have always sold premium pages. Television has operated, since its post-sponsorship days, on the basis of equal availability for all advertisers. In sports, however, the concept of exclusivity and advantageous positioning has been well developed. Anheuser-Busch effectively locked Miller and other competitors out of ESPN's major sports programming in its first several years by establishing an exclusive long-term agreement.

In the next section of *Adbashing,* I offer specific ideas for achieving media dominance. I identify emerging media and suggest several new opportunities that will change the way you think of advertising.

RESTRUCTURING THE TRANSACTIONAL
SEQUENCE OF NETWORK TELEVISION BUYING

Achieving significantly higher levels of frequency requires a complete rethinking of traditional media strategies. It means a return to program sponsorships on network television. Sponsorships are not necessarily full 100% sponsorships, but partial sponsorships with week-to-week identifiable continuity within the same programs. *Find the audience that buys your product and stick with them. Own them.*

Whether it is for sponsorship purposes or not, many advertisers are seeking to rewrite their traditional approaches to network spending. General Motors, under the guidance of Phil Guarascio, has developed unique relationships with Hollywood TV studios and broadcast networks to assist in the funding of certain programs, in return for advantageous network pricing. One GM deal enabled the network to produce its late night hit, *Bodies of Evidence*, a part of the *Crime Time After Prime Time* series constructed by CBS' Late Night guru, Rod Perth. Procter & Gamble media chief Jim Van Cleave is credited by CBS for his involvement in providing upfront funding for the initial production run of *Northern Exposure*. CBS agreed to commit inventory to P&G in return for their partial funding of the production for six Summer episodes. The program, which otherwise may never have been produced, has gone on to become a major hit series for CBS.

The single most spoken word in Hollywood production circles today is "deficit." Neither CBS nor NBC networks were profitable in 1992 and an increasing percentage of network prime time programs are unprofitable for the networks, the studios and the producers.

Therefore, the key issue for all those involved in new network productions is "who will cover the deficit." Profits depend upon hits. But fewer than two prime time programs out of every ten are hits. These few hits generate the revenues required to cover the deficits on all other programs. This "deficit funding" has centered production of prime time series at the major Hollywood studios such as Paramount, MCA/Universal and Disney. But now, even the profits of hit shows are eroding. Because audiences now have many viewing choices among four broadcast networks, basic cable, pay, pay-per-view and home video, there are fewer big hits. The syndication market, where the studios sell their hit network series to local TV stations for airing outside of prime time hours, is less profitable than it once was. Stations are investing in breakthrough original programs such as *Star Trek: Deep Space Nine, Star Trek: The Next Generation,* and *The Untouchables.* They are balancing these costs with relatively inexpensive movie packages, talk shows and low cost off-network shows.

Profits from hit shows are also being reduced by the decreased dependence of international programmers on product from the United States. Programmers in Europe, South America and the Pacific Rim have reduced their commitments to U.S. produced programs.

Studios, faced with increasing deficits, are asking whether they can afford to continue in the television programming business. Advertisers are looking to reduce the costs of network advertising. Independent producers are seeking opportunities to cover their costs without the studio as their partner. Networks, for their part, have been looking forward to the inevitable collapse of federally imposed financial interest rules, which prevent them from having "back end" ownership of network programs.

The abolishment of these rules by the FCC will coincide with a collapse of the "back end" market. Networks must find new ways of developing high quality prime time programming without spending the nearly $5 billion annually that this process consumes. It has become apparent that the process of funding network prime time programming cannot continue to operate on the basis of deficit spending and network losses. It must change, and this represents an opportunity for advertisers.

During my analyses of major changes in the business of advertising, I discovered that a friend and associate, David Houle, was experiencing many of the same realities. In 1990, David created, along with newsman Bill Kurtis and the A&E Network, a 26-week series called *World In Action*. For the 1991-92 season, Houle, Kurtis and A&E created *Investigative Reports with Bill Kurtis* and, subsequently, a second series, *American Justice*. Houle is the executive producer of *Energy Express*, a children's sports, health and fitness program that began its national roll-out on WGN-TV in early 1993. Houle's involvement in the network, syndication and international markets convinced him that the future of broadcast network prime time programming belonged to those talented producers who could deliver network quality dramas, sitcoms, movies and reality programs at significantly lower costs.

Houle and I spent hours together reviewing the depressing realities of a huge business that seemed to be following a script written by the American automotive industry in the 1970s. When faced with imported Japanese cars, Detroit's big three responded with business as usual. "Big cars, big profits; small cars, no profits" was their motto. Today, in Hollywood, the thinking is "big shows, big profits; small shows, no profits." But the reality is that huge losses are being suffered in the network and programming marketplace. High quality delivered for an affordable price is the future. Change is inevitable.

After speaking with major network advertisers, independent producers, studios and network executives, it became obvious that their common interests could be served by a restructured method of conducting business that would offer all parties increased stability, not radical change. To accomplish this end, Houle and I formed Television Production Partners, Inc. in 1992.

Television Production Partners represents the programming and production community, major national advertisers and the broadcast networks, working to assure a constant flow of quality programming within a cost structure that is viable for all parties.

Through the TPP funding model, a consortium of major network advertisers provide networks with the resources to initiate new and innovative approaches to reducing program costs while maintaining quality. Advertisers buy time in traditional ways at reduced costs, but offer flexibility to networks that allow program development fees to be eliminated. The bottom line is to increase network profitability, enabling them to reinvest in programming and promotion to increase ratings. It shifts the no-win formula which is in place today to a scenario where everyone wins -- advertisers, networks and producers.

Across all media we are witnessing a dramatic shift in traditional relationships. Those companies that best understand the business needs of all players, effectively manage the changing environment, assure a constant flow of money and profits and, thereby, maximize stability within the industry, will be those to whom the future belongs.

MAGAZINE SELECTIVE BINDING

Expanded niche targeting of audiences is clearly the highest priority for marketers in the 1990s and beyond. Hundreds of magazines have come onto the scene during the past several years serving very narrow audiences. Now magazines are offering even greater targeting capabilities through selective binding and ink-jet technologies.

Selective binding enables printers to select highly targeted groups of a magazine's subscribers, based upon any number of characteristics (such as geographic location, income, etc.) and bind special editorial and advertising sections only into the magazines being mailed to these groups. It allows advertisers to segment a magazine's circulation and customize advertising according to the unique demographics and psychographics of the reader.

Ink-jet technology allows publishers and advertisers to customize a personalized message to each individual subscriber. When I open my subscription to *Time* and see a special message welcoming me to the issue *by name,* I'm (hopefully) impressed. These combined technologies should create a marriage of direct marketing and magazines, ideally giving marketers tremendous benefits and shifting dollars from direct marketing back into traditional media advertising.

The major drawback to date of both selective binding and ink-jetting has been the cost. Magazines offering these capabilities, most visibly the Time Inc. magazines, have been met with demands that their costs conform to traditional advertising rather than direct marketing costs with magazine premiums.

Advertisers, while enthusiastic, have not aggressively developed marketing programs to test and develop these capabilities. Ad agency media departments have not been pressured by their clients to create special uses and have approached their negotiations with magazine companies with an attitude that selective binding should be offered at little or no premium.

Selective binding and ink-jet capabilities assure marketers that they can increasingly use magazines in ways that are more aggressively promotional in nature. As marketers focus on means to increase the impact and dominance of their advertising, looking to generate measurable sales results, we can expect demand to grow for both selective binding and ink-jet technologies.

ADVERTORIALS AND CUSTOM TITLES

Leveraging the brand names and strong audience franchises of traditional media to the direct benefit of advertisers is an important marketing opportunity for advertisers. Later in this book, I describe the aggressive efforts of MTV, CBS, the New York Times Company and other media companies to take their consumer franchises on the road with a variety of mall tours. *Playboy* developed several custom publications: *Playboy Guide to Executive Success, Playboy Guide to Health & Fitness* and *Playboy Guide to Grooming and Fashion* are among them. The traditional approach to line extensions taken by marketers is equally appropriate for media companies. Several magazines offer similar line extensions.

Advertisers traditionally sought to capture the editorial reputation of a magazine and reader loyalty by cloning the editorial look and inserting a special advertising section into the magazine. Several countries regularly do this in the major business and travel magazines to promote business and tourism. Revlon's magazine, *Revlon: 60 Years of Unforgettable Beauty,* was polybagged with 765,000 newsstand copies of *Vogue* and was created by *Vogue's* business staff. Unlike an insert, which may appear in several publications and is developed exclusively by the advertiser, an advertorial or "outsert" is often developed with editorial assistance from a magazine and often duplicates the graphic design of the magazine in which it appears.

Most magazine editors have scorned advertorials as disruptive of the editorial/design flow of the magazine; they claim it may jeopardize the trust the readers place in the integrity of the editorial staff. *The New Yorker* Magazine, under Editor Tina Brown, has adopted the policy of rejecting all advertorials. The more credible a magazine's editorial and the more readers depend upon a magazine for advice and information, the more advertisers would want to associate themselves with that credibility.

Marketers will be well served by separating themselves from the editorial product, assuring that magazines continue to maintain their unique relationships with readers. Conversely, magazines will increasingly seek to leverage their reputations by developing appropriate means to communicate specific marketing messages in formats that carry with them the imprimatur of their style and editorial focus.

Whittle Communications has been successful with their *Special Reports*, specially developed magazines and books targeted for specific audiences with a single sponsor, or several non-competitive sponsors. Magazines will increasingly duplicate this concept, publishing special one-time supplements on a specific issue. These sponsored vehicles can be distributed via several alternative, highly targeted, channels. *Newsweek* custom-publishes several different versions of its weekly magazine, each with added editorial emphasis on particular issues, such as the *International Scene.* Subscribers identify the editorial focus in which they are most interested, and advertisers have the opportunity to tie their ads into this special section.

Marketers now must clearly identify their own goals and the best media vehicles to communicate them. They will examine closely the editorial positioning of all magazines reaching their target audiences and determine which have the greatest reader loyalty and involvement. The opportunity to identify with these magazines and, by association, with their audiences, will be a primary media and creative goal. Opportunities to build unique channels of distribution will be equally important. I expect companies such as Mary Kay Cosmetics, Tupperware and Avon will become distributors of specially developed magazines that feature non-competitive advertisers. Sales representatives will not only sell the publications, but also personally deliver and review each issue, pointing out coupons, special offers and highlighted editorial. We can expect to find sponsored special issues of magazines at our airplane seats, in our health clubs, at our supermarkets, and mailed to our offices.

Assuring maximum marketing effectiveness requires that media and marketers form a team for distribution and promotion of their specially created advertorials. They must be partners.

The burden of developing, promoting and selling fresh new concepts of media creativity has historically been on media companies. The agency's role has been to analyze and recommend. An endless selling process and low success rate has resulted in a dearth of bright, new ideas. Marketers and ad agencies, in the future, will take a more aggressive approach in developing and bringing new ideas to media companies. Those media companies that embrace and expand upon their advertisers' concepts are those that will thrive in the 1990s.

NEWSPAPERS FINALLY REACT

The newspaper industry, which virtually *created* the advertising industry, has, until recently, steadfastly refused to adapt and respond to the dramatic changes in that industry. The advertising industry owes a great debt to the early newspaper barons who understood the connection between their readers and their advertisers, and who made the selling of their advertisers' goods and services their top priority.

Newspapers, for the past 30 years, have not responded effectively to the competition of radio, television and, increasingly, cable. Newspapers are primarily a local medium. Because they continue to be a dominant advertising vehicle for the retailing industry, newspapers still command the lion's share of ad spending (nearly 50%). But retail spending is on the decline. Major national retailers such as Kmart, JCPenney and Wal-Mart displaced mom & pop stores for whom newspapers was a dominant medium. These national chains are more dependent upon national media. Direct-to-the-home circular distribution has become more efficient than inserting circulars in newspapers.

There are far fewer newspapers today than there were in the 1940s, pre-television. In many cities, even the one surviving daily newspaper is unprofitable.

Newspapers were largely ignored by national advertisers because of difficulties in dealing with multiple sizes and formats, the lack of electronic delivery systems and pricing systems that penalized the national advertiser. For the 1990s, Cathie Black, president of the Newspaper Association of America, admits that "Newspapers *must* adapt and change for a radically different world. This is the decade of the customer. We have to serve our customers better -- both readers and advertisers. We must be responsive to what [advertisers] want and need."

For their part, marketers are eager for the newspaper industry to be more responsive and focused on national standardization. Elimination of the national vs. retail rate is an essential paradigm shift that is certain to have positive repercussions on newspapers' national advertising support. Size standardization and satellite delivery of advertising also will have a positive impact on the industry.

The advantage that newspapers offer is primarily the ability to communicate different messages with immediate daily changes and local variations. This is especially relevant for industries such as entertainment, travel, financial services and automotive. Black suggests that "a dazzling array of technology in the newspaper plant itself allows us to offer advertisers the same targeting and direct response capabilities of other media. Within the next five years, newspaper advertisers will be able to deliver their message to a select group of subscribers. And not too far in the future, subscribers will be able to choose the sections of the paper they want." Newspapers also have developed sampling capabilities that enable advertisers to distribute free products to selected readers along with their Sunday papers.

The success of *USA Today* has had an important impact on the newspaper industry, influencing not only the graphic look but the content of many papers. Many of *USA Today's* steady advertisers use interactive techniques and successfully generate direct reader response.

USA Today is attracting a new base of national advertisers to the newspaper medium, educating them in new ways to achieve sales results with the most traditional of advertising media. Paul Mulcahy, formerly Vice President of Marketing for Campbell Soup Company, tells of his desire to place special rainy day ads in selected newspapers, but the industry was unwilling (or unable) to offer the flexibility of running the ads only when rain was in the forecast. Simon Kornblit, Executive Vice President of Universal Pictures, has attempted to work closely with the newspaper industry to implement unique media executions intended to draw attention to specific films' advertising.

Kornblit reports that until recently the industry was unresponsive, but now has begun breaking down its intransigence in the face of change. In this light, both marketers and readers can begin to see more creative and innovative uses of the newspaper medium. As weekly shoppers become a more mainstream medium, they will enhance the value of newspaper advertising and lead the industry back toward growth and expansion.

Some experts believe that computers will take over the role of newspapers as a primary delivery system for daily in-depth news and information. The experiences of previous attempts by Knight-Ridder, Times-Mirror and others to introduce computer-based Videotext information systems suggest otherwise.

While computers will most certainly become more user-friendly, the newspaper and other print media will continue to be viable delivery systems into the foreseeable future. The challenge is to adapt to a more electronically oriented marketing environment and take better advantage of technology to serve both audiences and advertisers.

THE INTERCONNECTED SOCIETY

Many of the future opportunities for marketers revolve around the growth of interactive capabilities. Full interactivity exists today in the form of the telephone. The first step in interactivity -- merging television and telephone technologies -- has been in place for years but has been underutilized by America's marketers. A primary reason for this is telephone lines cannot handle the large volume of calls television advertising can generate.

But direct response advertisers, the two-minute sellers of everything from Time-Life Books to Hank Williams' albums and Ginsu Knives, have long understood the potential of lower rated cable television and local independent television stations. As far back as 1970, local telephone companies were developing the capacity to handle huge call volume, anticipating an increase in television-telephone interactivity. Many major telemarketing firms are headquartered in Omaha because of the advanced capacity capabilities developed there by U.S. West.

With fiber optic wiring and cable, plus increased telephone company involvement in programming distribution, the trend toward interactivity will continue. Sony Pictures Entertainment and United Video Group are launching The Game Show Channel, taking advantage of the new interactive television technology that will enable viewers to participate in the televised game show activities. United Video, which distributes to local cable systems Superstation WGN-TV and the Prevue Channel, will provide marketing, distribution and technological support. Sony's Columbia Pictures TV Group will develop the programming.

A second Game Show Network is being launched by The Family

Channcl, one of the earliest cable networks (originally Christian Broadcasting Network). The Game Show Channel will use 900# interactive technology to attract viewers/contestants throughout the programming day. Games will cover a range of topics such as sports, movies, music, history and news.

GTE and Philips Electronics are co-developing a new type of interactive television, which combines broadcast TV with computer-based interactive compact discs. This two-way system sends encoded television signals to Philips CD-1 sets, allowing consumers to order products, vote, participate in game shows, etc.

Time-Warner and IBM have explored an alliance to link IBM's technology with Time-Warner's extensive library of movies, television shows and cable television capabilities. The early emphasis would be on pay-per-view movies. Video-on-demand to the home is a computer-intensive technology that currently is in use. The new technologies utilize interactivity in real-time, enhancing the power and immediacy of pay-per-view and allowing viewers to participate live with a variety of programs.

TV Answer, developed by manufacturer Hewlett-Packard, is committed to placing 1.5 million interactive wireless television appliances into homes in 1993. TV Answer is a licensed Federal Communications Commission low-power television service promising to provide viewers with low-cost interactive services, including programming, check-paying, games, information, etc. Most observers consider it the least likely to succeed of the emerging interactive technologies, primarily because of its dependence upon a franchised distribution format.

LeGroup Videotron's Videoway service has been underway in Montreal for several years and is now being expanded to Ottawa, the

United States, England, and Denmark. The U.S. version, developed and marketed by ACTV, has received resistance from cable television operators but interest from marketers and programmers. Two hundred thousand subscribers in Montreal use the system. It gives viewers access to more than 100 data services, animated video games, electronic mail, broadcast teletext, electronic magazine and newspaper services, home shopping and banking, PC modem communications, video cataloging, couponing and audience metering. Its most appealing services, in addition to PPV movies, are interactive capabilities that allow viewers to choose camera angles in live sports or concert events. A weekly lottery game asks subscribers to deposit up to $20 for the right to receive a series of numbers delivered electronically to their screens, which are matched to winning numbers when they are drawn on the live program.

Many of these programs are reminiscent of an early cable effort, UTV Network, which was in development from 1980 - 1982, but did not receive sufficient support from the cable industry to launch its interactive programming services. The UTV Network, which I joined in 1982 as executive vice president after leaving CBS, was created by Frank D'Allesio who had made several million dollars building and selling cable television systems in New Jersey.

D'Allesio's concept was that the telephone and the television represented a logical combination which could be exploited by creating programming for mass audiences. The distribution limitations of cable in 1982 worked to UTV's favor, since they allowed the network's distribution to grow along with telephone trunk line capacity.

UTV, in 1982, was negotiating with Sears to create the first home shopping network, a daily three hour - five hour late-night and weekend programming block. We were discussing with program creator Chuck Barris a live version of *The Dating Game*, which would allow viewers to call in and select the dating partner. The *New Gong Show* permitted viewers to call-in and, when enough calls accumulated, gong the talent. Existing telephone hardware created a real-time capability for tracking calls. A lottery show called *Super-Ringo* was successfully tested on the Suburban Cable System in New Jersey with host John Kerr, and planned for national UTV roll-out with retailer tie-ins. Steve Allen was signed for a weekly new age and jazz music show with live calls from viewers to talk to the guests. A Larry King-type call-in talk program, soap operas, business shows, sports gambling shows, sports talk and much more were all on the boards for development.

UTV's vision was that the cable industry would fund the development of programming and distribution, attracting viewers to the programming and the 800# interactive participation. Once 900# technologies were developed and home shopping fulfillment capabilities expanded, UTV would begin feeding tremendous revenues back to the cable operators. UTV would have been a completely viewer funded network and its mass appeal, we believed, would have also made it one of the most popular.

Unfortunately for D'Allesio, who lost several million dollars on the venture, UTV was seeking financial support at the same time that CBS developed and then bailed out of CBS Cable, a channel featuring costly cultural programming. CBS's highly visible failure made banks and capital sources very wary of cable networks. Although cable today appears to have been a "no brainer" for financial sources, in 1982 cable programming was considered a significant risk. Although several entrepreneurs successfully began cable networks, cable lost its best opportunity to establish a huge revenue stream through the early development of programming designed to drive usage of 900# interactivity.

In the 1990s and beyond, several marketers are aggressively developing interactivity via both the telephone and new technologies. For advertisers, the best opportunities continue to be driven by the natural affinity between television and telephone, and investments in programming combining these technologies are the most likely to succeed. The technology that dramatically alters this relationship in the longer-term is the computer and computer-like capabilities made possible by fiber optics.

Lucie Fjeldstad, an IBM vice president, feels this combination creates a whole new industry. She recently told the Associated Press that IBM sees "four industries converging: computers, consumer electronics, telecommunications, and media and entertainment, to form a new industry that will deliver a wide spectrum of digital goods and services to businesses and homes."

Rick Parkhill, president of *Response TV* Magazine, believes that "This convergence of technology may add up to a new industry for vendors like IBM, but for media and marketing people it represents the most significant evolutionary stride in media since the printing press. Think of it -- media that communicates two ways, invites involvement, and personalizes the information and entertainment consumers choose to receive."

The best known and most successful of the computer-based information services is Prodigy, a joint venture of Sears and IBM. CBS was an original partner, but dropped out in the mid-1980s. Prodigy began 1993 with nearly 1.5 million subscribers paying on a usage basis. The service is not considered a significant vehicle for home shopping, as had been originally expected, but it currently has more than 200 advertisers on-line, about one-third of them national. Chevrolet recently offered a $500 bonus rebate on its GEO model to Prodigy subscribers. Those who requested the rebate on-line received a postcard at home a few weeks later from the local dealership reminding them to come in for a test drive. Travel, financial services and other information-intensive marketers are natural Prodigy advertisers.

Other similar services include H&R Block's CompuServe and smaller services -- GEnie, Delphi and America Online.

Advertisers hoping to reap the rewards of computer interactivity must recognize it is a different medium from any other and develop their communications accordingly. The messages must be enhanced by the interactive capability and be responsive to the reality that the customer views the computer as a highly personal, involving and service-intensive medium. *Direct* Magazine comments that "Once customers get on an electronic network their expectations grow exponentially. They 'grow long nails and hair on their hands,' warns William Tobin, president of PC Flowers, which launched its floral delivery business on Prodigy. 'They tell you when you really didn't do a good job, and they want your firstborn back for it.'"

DMB&B's *Media Insights* newsletter accurately summed up the impact of interactivity:

"Media and society are in the midst of a radical shift from an era of mass media transmitted by air to an era of class media transmitted by wire. Mass media let advertisers address masses of consumers at a time. Class media will let individual consumers and advertisers interact. The prototypical mass medium is broadcasting; the prototypical class medium is the telephone. The class media of the future (be they telephone, cable or some combination of the two) will convey words, numbers and images as well as voices in huge quantities over hundreds of thousands of channels.

"Mass media are associated with passive audiences, mass production and mass consumption. As the media shift from mass to class, a new social character and new means of productions and consumption will emerge. The nature of these new media may even affect the type of products produced. Mass marketers' success is due in part to their skilled use of mass media, which, consciously or not, also affect their product development. The exact nature of class media society is impossible to predict. We do know it will be stratified in terms of consumers' and advertisers' ability to participate."

ZAPPERS TAKE CONTROL

The most basic form of television interactivity is reflected in the relationship of television viewers with their newest device of convenience: the remote control, more commonly referred to as the *zapper*. *TV Guide* recently wrote that future earth archeologists will conclude that "20th Century America's primary tool was not the computer, the car, or even the telephone, but a humble jumble of buttons called the *remote.*"

The first TV with a wireless remote device was introduced by Zenith in 1956, bearing the name *Space Command.* An immediate hit, the Zenith innovation is now a standard necessity in homes with cable television and a multi-channel environment. Eighty-five percent of all homes have one or more remote controls.

While critics used to say that television viewers made forced program choices based upon the "least objectionable program" available to them, the remote control has created the exciting opportunity for viewers to rapidly scan myriad choices available to them and select the *most desirable program.* This represents a radical change for viewers, programmers and advertisers.

The growth of cable networks has resulted directly from viewers' willingness to scan their programming choices and has created obvious, and relatively traditional advertising opportunities for marketers with cable networks. The success of cable heralds another new opportunity that marketers have just begun to acknowledge.

In the earliest days of television, NBC was the dominant network, featuring the known stars and the most station affiliates. When CBS raided NBC and captured stars like Jack Benny, loyalties shifted. CBS generated even stronger viewer loyalties through its news leadership with Edward R. Morrow and Walter Cronkite. In the 1970s, ABC was the first network to target younger viewers, breaking CBS's stranglehold on first place in prime time ratings in 1976-77 with programs such as *Happy Days, Laverne & Shirley, Charlie's Angels, The Six Million Dollar Man,* and the breakthrough mini-series, *Rich Man, Poor Man* and *Roots.*

Networks learned that brand loyalty toward broadcast networks could not be depended upon to hold viewers. A favorite comment in network and ad circles was (and still is) "people watch programs, not networks." Basically, that is true. But, in the new network environment, *network* loyalty can be a factor in leading viewers to particular *programs.* Cable News Network, MTV, Lifetime, USA, The Family Channel, Arts & Entertainment and The Discovery Channel prove that point every day. Fox Network proved that the same could happen with a broadcast network.

When Fox launched in 1986, it first set out to create programs that had a clear and *consistent* image and target audience -- youth. Fox then co-opted that youth audience and image as its own. Subsequent Fox Network programs had the imprimatur of the network's image, assuring that fans of other Fox programs would be receptive to sampling Fox's new offerings.

The marginal success of *21 Jump Street,* combined with the tremendous popularity of *The Simpson's* and *In Living Color* helped to attract audiences to Fox's biggest success, *Beverly Hills 90210.* That success, in turn, helped to launch *Melrose Place*, which has become a marginal Fox hit.

The successes of *90210* and *Melrose Place* hold an interesting ironic twist of fate. Aaron Spelling, the producer of both programs, has been a consistently successful independent producer since 1960 when he launched *Zane Grey Theater*. He followed with *Burke's Law, Mod Squad, The Rookies, The Smothers Brothers Show, Family* and *Charlie's Angels*. Spelling was one of the primary contributors to ABC's success in the 1970s and was given an exclusive contract to develop programs for the network into the 1980s. In Ken Auletta's *Three Blind Mice,* which tracks the fates of the three major broadcast networks, Spelling's career and his fall from favor at the networks and, subsequently, in the Hollywood community, is charted in graphic detail. At the end of Auletta's book, NBC's failure with Spelling's *Nightingales* appears to spell his doom as a Hollywood power.

Today, Spelling's career is not only redeemed, but is at its peak, thanks to Fox's ability to provide audience sampling and an environment supportive of programs targeted to young audiences. While Fox's continued success is only as strong as its continued ability to produce appealing programming, Fox itself has developed an aura and identity among its program's loyal audiences.

CBS, while not building an identity to equal Fox's, is a leader on two fronts: sports and programs targeted to a 25-54 audience. This is more of a ratings tactic than a strategic marketing plan on CBS' part, but it demonstrates leadership none the less.

MTV Networks Inc. was the first company to recognize the marketing opportunities inherent in building a brand identity for its networks. MTV and Nickelodeon licensed their names for products ranging from clothing to trading cards. Nickelodeon opened their own studio tour at Universal Studios in Orlando, offering visitors a chance to appear on a Nickelodeon show and chat with network stars like Ren & Stimpy.

Beverly Hills 90210 and *The Simpson's* have licensed products based on the programs' characters, but the licensing value of the MTV and Nickelodeon names transcends traditional program and character licensing. CNN, ESPN, The Discovery Channel, Sci-Fi Channel and Comedy Central represent similar opportunities.

The issue for these networks, as well as Fox, is where the line between capitalizing on equity value in their name and gross commercialism is crossed. Marketers have the opportunity, right now, to seek relationships which allow them the rights to align their products with these networks' identities. If *Batman* can have a cereal, can a *Nickelodeon* brand be far behind? We have *90210* and *All My Children* trading cards. Is an *MTV* candy bar feasible. MTV and Visa explored a relationship in which Visa would become the exclusive credit card of MTV. Why not an *MTV Museum of Youth Culture* sponsored by Coca-Cola or Pepsi Cola and other appropriate marketers. MTV's traveling *Museum of Unnatural History* mall tour launched in 1988 was the first step in this process of aligning marketers with the medium.

Networks have always found a market in labeled apparel, especially sports apparel with the ESPN or CBS Sports logo. Arts & Entertainment and The Discovery Channel offer subscriptions to their magazines; several networks are marketing videos. Networks have the opportunity to develop brand identities that in turn can be used to expand their value to advertisers.

The A&E Viewers Club will offer data base and direct marketing capabilities for A&E advertisers. Networks such as Comedy Central, Sci-Fi Channel and E!, as they grow, can develop associations that strengthen their ties with viewers and offer greater value to advertisers. These networks will be well served by hiring marketing executives such as CBS' George Schweitzer, NBC's Alan Cohen, and ABC's Peter Chrisanthopoulos who understand how brand loyalty can be achieved, translated into product line extensions, and then converted into opportunities for network advertisers.

CBS is particularly aggressive in taking their programming and sponsors "on-the-road" with mall tours. "Women...On Style...On Fitness...On Family," a tour of 25 major market shopping malls began in January 1993. The tour is a joint effort by CBS, *Family Circle* and *McCall's*. Highlights of the tour include appearances by magazine editors and personalities from CBS programs. Interactive displays on beauty, fashion, fitness and health are featured. CBS also sponsors college and mall tours focused on sports and soap operas.

The combination of brand loyalty, program allegiance and interactivity creates a powerful tool for advertisers. It is one of the key opportunities to reverse the 20 year slide of marketing budgets from media advertising to direct marketing and sales promotion.

Just as corporations are recognizing the importance of investing in programs that establish and maintain brand equity, they are also recognizing the importance of building relationships with those companies responsible for communicating brand messages to their customers. Media companies, in the future, will be more valued when they are marketing partners, involved with the advertiser's objectives and goals and capable of lending their own unique identity to a marketer's cause.

ELECTRONIC RETAILING -- HOME SHOPPING NETWORKS

I've been fascinated as I've watched the growth of the cable home shopping phenomenon throughout the 1980s and '90s. This must be one of the most silent $2.2 billion dollar businesses in marketing. Home Shopping Network and QVC Shopping Network, either alone or together, are available in a large majority of U.S. homes via cable and broadcast stations. Both QVC and HSN offer second networks, along with a fashion shopping network. Liberty Media was the best cable stock of 1992 and capped the year with increased ownership of HSN and QVC. Barry Diller, recognized as one of the most talented executives in the entertainment industry and the man who built Fox Network, has jumped on the bandwagon with a $25 million investment in QVC. Turner and Whittle veteran Gerry Hogan, President of HSN, rounds out a talent pool unprecedented in the cable or broadcasting industry.

HSN and QVC sell merchandise 24 hours a day, live! HSN's telephone service center has more than 23,000 operational telephone lines with more than 2,500 live operators, fielding more than 300,000 inbound calls daily with the capacity to handle more than two million calls a day. HSN ships an average of 72,000 packages per day, or more than 26 million items per year.

More than just shopping networks, they are pretty good talk shows as well. During any given week Joan Rivers will spend several hours discussing many topics, while callers purchase her line of jewelry on QVC. Marie Osmond promotes her ceramic dolls that sell for up to $800 each; Susan Lucci promotes her line of cosmetics; and Richard Simmons sells *Deal-a-Meal*. The Say-Hey Kid, Willie Mays, might guest host a Sports Memorabilia Hour, reminiscing while callers ask him questions and, of course, purchase an item or two. Other on-screen promoters include Frankie Avalon, Connie Stevens and Robin Leach.

Gold and cubic zirconium remain a staple on the home shopping networks, but there is variety and, surprise, entertainment for the channel grazer. HSN and QVC consider their viewers to be more than just an audience. They are members, with a membership card and an opportunity to win prizes just by viewing. But they are also friends. Program hosts are on a first name basis with regular callers. When a caller is absent for a few weeks, other callers ask after his or her health, and perhaps an outbound call may be made to see how they're doing. The shopping networks are a community of television viewers, bound together by live, interactive television.

Critic David Bazelon in 1966 recognized the reality and importance of television as a community:

"Our popular culture, now centered around television, will always be deeply compelling because it is our only community.... The factor to reckon with here is that genuine community cannot be elitist: community reaches to the limits of identification."

For many people, Home Shopping Network and QVC, and their hosts, are the Arthur Godfrey of the 1990s -- they are welcome guests in their homes. In the earlier days of television, Godfrey, Milton Berle, Sid Caesar, Dave Garroway of *Today*, Steve Allen and even Johnny Carson would thank their viewers "for letting them be guests in their homes." Today, we hear that comment very rarely. But on HSN and QVC we hear it quite often and it's addressed to individuals. "Thank you for calling," "Thank you for watching," and "Thank you for purchasing" are the most heard words. (This lesson has not been lost on the broadcast networks; CBS has been thanking its audience for watching and for making CBS the most viewed network in America.)

Into this environment enter companies selling their products. Not the brand names found in traditional retail stores, but still backed by a guarantee and assurances of lowest costs. Traditional marketers have not yet discovered the potential of the home shopping empires, often fearful of retailer reaction. But as retailers seek to increase their influence and clout -- and their profits -- at the expense of consumers and the manufacturers, we can expect major corporations to discover this new media opportunity.

In a 150 channel environment, will it be a surprise to find a food channel, devoted to recipes and the direct sales of food products, cooking utensils (beyond the Bamboo Steamer, Ginsu Knife and Wok set), and other peripheral items? In this environment, Kraft General Foods, Procter & Gamble, Nabisco, Campbell Soup and others can develop their own 30 minute - 60 minute programs to communicate directly with consumers and market products to them.

Not too far in the distant future, we can expect a medical network to be created for broad audiences. Today, Lifetime Network provides a one-day-a-week service for the medical profession, while Whittle Communications pipes programming into doctors' offices for both the doctors and their patients. Will it be long before a similar network is provided over America's cable systems? Viewers not only will learn about medical discoveries and have the opportunity to have common ailments diagnosed, but also will be able to order prescriptions directly from a central source. Direct mail prescriptions already exist, so televised programming to support them cannot be far behind.

The travel industry has The Travel Channel, recently purchased and expanded by Landmark Communications, owner of the Weather Channel. A future channel could be the 800# Services Channel, brought to you by AT&T in support of the many companies who offer products via 800# service. Program vignettes about these companies and their products could easily fill a 24-hour day. The costs of the network would be paid by the companies using 800 numbers based upon a percentage of the calls generated to them, providing revenues to cable systems and thereby reducing cable fees, increasing AT&T 800# usage, and increasing the profitability of the many companies that rely upon the telephone as a primary source of revenues.

An automotive network is more than a possibility -- it is very likely that the success of and interest in auto racing and auto buff books will extend to rapid expansion of television programming targeted not only to enthusiasts but to all those who are in the market for cars. Imagine the next time you're in the market for a new car, turning on your television set and simply requesting a series of programs on models selected to meet your requirements and specifications.

Robert Pittman, CEO of Time-Warner Enterprises and one of the innovators who developed MTV, describes the dawning age of "smart TV:"

> "If you're looking for a ski parka, basically you tell your TV you're looking for a ski parka, it'll go through 50 digitized catalogs, pick them all out for you and let you choose the type of shell, in blue or red, and it will show you pictures."

ELECTRONIC RETAILING -- INFOMERCIALS

The 800# concept of promoting individual companies and products for direct purchase via an 800 telephone number is a spin-off of the hugely successful infomercial business, which today generates over three-quarters of a billion dollars in revenues. Companies such as Regal Corporation of Pennsylvania and National Media Corp. produce hundreds of 30-minute programs each year, marketing products ranging from Anushka's anti-cellulite products and Edgar Morris' Skin Care treatments for Afro-Americans to Karaoke Classics and the Great Wok of China. Over 100,000 hours of broadcast and cable network time are purchased annually for these programs.

Many infomercials feature stars who talk about their use of the product. These stars include Cher, Martin Sheen, Bruce Jenner, Kenny Rogers, Mary Ann Mobley and football legend Fran Tarkenton. Regal has purchased all rights to Joan Rivers' products and is extending her QVC home shopping franchise to infomercials. Infomercials have become so successful in selling products that several traditional marketers are looking to the format as an alternative to traditional retail and direct marketing distribution. Both General Motors (for Saturn) and Volvo have used the 30-minute format to promote their products, offering information via an 800# rather than enabling viewers to make a direct purchase. Traditional advertising agencies such as Saatchi & Saatchi are exploring opportunities to develop infomercials for their traditional advertising clients.

Home Shopping Network Entertainment Inc., a subsidiary of HSN, runs a 24-hour infomercial network and foresees "a commercial market among Fortune 1000 corporations and advertising agencies."

HSNE envisions that these infomercials "will promote corporate identity, brands, products and services [via] Corporate Showcase Videos." Slow to get off the ground, the infomercial network is an idea whose time has yet to come.

Infomercials, especially with the expansion of cable television networks, have a bright future in the television landscape. The goal of traditional manufacturers should be to maintain the skills and unique qualities of the infomercial and apply them to selling their products, rather than attempting to conform the infomercial style to traditional marketing techniques.

The danger of traditional marketers such as General Motors and Volvo entering the infomercial arena is their marketing priorities are often not complimentary to the style and format that drives successful consumer motivation. These companies have so much invested in product image advertising that they do not necessarily convert their marketing messages into infomercials, which are much more pointed and direct in nature.

IBM marketing head James Reilly was quoted in *Business Week* as saying the infomercial industry "is overcoming its earlier reputation as a fringe marketing option." Companies as diverse as AT&T, Avon and Sears are exploring infomercials, while Time-Life, Black & Decker, Corning, Pearle Vision Centers and Burger King have aired them.

Infomercials have been successful because their primary goal has been "one-stop selling." When the primary goal becomes lead generation rather than direct product sales, the value and interest to consumers is diminished. Success for traditional marketers will require that they confront their existing distribution resources or develop new product lines specifically for direct distribution.

Major advertisers are also accustomed to placing their messages in prime time and key dayparts, where infomercials rarely appear. Many companies may fear that an association with infomercials and lesser dayparts may somehow stain their image. Rather, it is more likely that their presence will elevate the perception of infomercials among viewers. Broadcast networks ABC, CBS, NBC and Fox are all expected to develop programming that clones the infomercial format, increasing credibility of infomercials as a marketing tool. A willing suspension of traditional attitudes toward advertising as an image-building or lead-generation vehicle will be necessary before brand name marketers will be successful with infomercials. Infomercials will not be appropriate for many advertisers for these reasons. Those who move to this new format and adjust their strategies accordingly rather than trying to adapt the format to their traditional marketing techniques, will be very successful.

THE MARKET RESEARCH CHANNEL

Imagine the opportunities inherent in an interactive television network that does nothing but ask its audience marketing questions day-in and day-out. Imagine further that researchers can call consumers and request that they respond to a particular marketing test appearing at a specific time and compensate them accordingly, addressing issues of sample composition.

Can the marketing research industry adjust to televised research, changing the very dynamic of the nature of the questioning process from print to video? The opportunity exists to do just this. Perhaps this concept will be integrated into networks such as CNBC or the "food" channel discussed earlier.

Broadcast networks have created similar "interactive" programs, giving viewers the opportunity to participate in the "Auto Safety Test" or the "Is Your Marriage Happy?" test. But with the realities of interactive television and computer/television hook-ups upon us, viewers will have the ability to actually respond and have their opinions tabulated.

Several broadcast networks, stations and cable networks have promoted an 800# and 900# on a one-time basis to identify viewer attitudes toward political issues or other concerns relevant to the moment. Twenty thousand people responded to a 900# aired during the Arsenio Hall Show on late night TV, raising over $10,000 for AIDS-related charities. Hall asked his viewers to pay 95 cents to vote whether they liked the "younger, darker" Michael Jackson or the "older, lighter" Jackson. (Seventy-five percent preferred the older, lighter entertainer.)

The message is that people *are* willing to respond. We also know from the success of infomercials and shopping networks that their interest in television is not strictly limited to entertainment, sports and news. They welcome the opportunity to respond. With well packaged, meaningful video marketing research, marketers will have the opportunity to bring expensive marketing research techniques directly into the home. If well done, this will begin to bridge the manufacturer/retailer information gap, returning the power of information to manufacturers.

There are, of course, obstacles to this concept as there are to all new ideas, but resourceful marketers are certain to hurdle these obstacles if the opportunity exists to develop a radically new resource for gaining direct feedback from consumers.

BETTY CROCKER IS A REAL PERSON!

The idea of infomercials is not new. While traditional packaged goods marketers may be the last to jump on the infomercial bandwagon in the 1990s, they were the first to develop the genre as far back as 1950 when *The Betty Crocker Television Show* aired on CBS. As I have discussed earlier, advertising agencies will be more valued by marketers when they can assist in converting marketing objectives into communications objectives, fully integrating all forms of communications into a single marketing execution. Infomercials are a starting point for this process.

As media companies seek ways to build their brand loyalty among consumers, marketers will also seek opportunities to extend their brand equity into new media forms. Donnelley Marketing's *New Age Directions* study conducted among the 50-64 age group found that Betty Crocker was the first or second choice of favorite spokesperson. Many believe she is a real person. This finding held constant in a separate study conducted among adults over 29 years old. The implication is that a Betty Crocker cooking show would have a built in audience and credibility, helping both the marketer and the network. Actually, Betty Crocker appeared on two ABC daytime shows in 1952: *Betty Crocker Star Matinee* and *Bride and Groom*. Ninety-seven percent of American women were able to recognize Betty Crocker by sight.

Donnelley Marketing has built a brand name identity for *Carol Wright*, the name under which it has distributed coupons to consumers for years. Now Donnelley plans to license the Carol Wright name and image. Carol Wright may soon be a cereal, or a branded name for produce. Will a Carol Wright television program follow?

The 1980s was the decade of athletes and performers as spokespeople. The trials and tribulations of many of these stars, and the growing threat of disclosure of drug and alcohol abuse, AIDS, homosexuality, political activism, etc. are causing a trend away from star endorsements. This makes fictional stars like Carol Wright all the more appealing.

General Motors has recognized the franchise in its own name and identity, and its opportunity to introduce new products using the General Motors cache and promotional tie-in clout. GM has extended its name to a credit card, as AT&T successfully did with the Universal Card. GM's card contributes a percentage of all purchases toward the purchase of a new GM car or truck.

As outlined above, AT&T could create a television program or network promoting its 800# users. Alex Karras, the well-known Detroit Lions' all-pro and star of the TV hit show *Webster,* has created a concept for a situation comedy taking place in an auto showroom, with products integrated into the program content. Cars become an integral part of the show and the automotive sponsor helps promote the TV show, in addition to the other way around.

Can we expect Hertz to sponsor its own travel program on The Travel Channel; or how about a prime time soap opera built around the life of a Mary Kay Cosmetics sales representative? Is this crass commercialism or an appropriate merger of need with opportunity? While critics would charge that commercial interests have gone too far, all they are really doing is returning to the roots that made them successful.

Television's early success as a commercial medium resulted from the strong association of programs with advertisers: *The Texaco Star Theater;* Chevrolet's sponsorship of *The Dinah Shore Show* and *Bonanza*; *The Chevy Show Starring Bob Hope*; *Mutual of Omaha's Wild Kingdom*; NBC's *Colgate Comedy Hour* helped launch the careers of Jerry Lewis and Dean Martin; *Coke Time with Eddie Fisher*; *Philco TV Playhouse*; the *G.E. College Bowl*; *Lucky Strike's Your Hit Parade*; *The Gillette Cavalcade of Sports* (Gillette was the first television sponsor with the telecast of the Joe Louis vs. Billy Conn boxing match, June 19, 1946); *Schlitz Playhouse of Stars* on CBS; the *Camel News Caravan* with John Cameron Swayze; *Lux Video Theater* (which started as Lux Radio Theater). And among those of us who grew up in the 1950s, who could forget *Captain Midnight* and the Ovaltine "secret squadron badges" and "code rings" that allowed us to actively participate with the program.

It was the availability of affiliations between advertisers and the medium that spurred television's early growth. As advertising demand grew, sponsorship became too expensive, except for the occasional *Hallmark Hall of Fame* or AT&T sponsored specials. The re-creation of these types of sponsorships and associations is not inappropriate since the loss of these opportunities changed the face of television advertising and diminished its inherent value to advertisers.

Within the current programming environment, it is both natural and appropriate that advertisers should once again seek to reestablish one of the television medium's greatest strengths. Marketers and the medium have come a long way since the 1950s; we can expect advertiser/media associations and relationships to be far more sophisticated and targeted. But the medium and the audience are more sophisticated as well.

Incidentally, for those who may think the Mary Kay concept is far fetched, consider this: The hit movie *Fried Green Tomatoes* features Kathy Bates as a housewife who becomes a Mary Kay consultant. Anyone who purchases a "previously viewed" version of the videotape from home video retailers is eligible for a free Mary Kay Cosmetics lipstick, valued at $9, and a free makeover from a local Mary Kay consultant. The company may also become involved in promoting cable distribution of the film.

ADVERTISING'S BACK-END -- RELIEVING THE PRESSURE

Hollywood studios are becoming far more sophisticated about the potential revenues to be generated from product insertion in films. Few producers and studios are willing or able to impose creative restrictions on filmmakers, but the traditional barriers are slowly being removed. One Hollywood consultant, Warren Weideman, is offering marketers the opportunity to be a dominant element of a new movie starring Alex Karras. The film is based upon Karras' novel *Tuesday Night Football,* which features a popular cult figure whose claim to fame is that he communicates almost totally with commercial slogans. While Karras' script is full of clever, albeit blatant, commercialism, it reflects the growing recognition by both talent and behind-the-scenes management that marketers offer an opportunity to relieve some of the pressures of increasing production costs, enabling them to maintain production quality.

Product placement goes well beyond the visible existence of products in films. It includes rights for extensive back-end marketing such as in-store tie-ins, in-theater promotion, home video advertising, newspaper advertising tie-ins, etc. The opportunities have just begun to be explored and tapped, with executives like Weideman pushing the meter in Hollywood and on Madison Avenue.

IT'S FREE

Actually putting your product into the hands of the consumer is considered the most effective means for gaining brand awareness and loyalty. Just as media need to attract readers and viewers for the first time, product manufacturers recognize that the first-time purchase is the most difficult. When resistance can be reduced through free distribution, a major obstacle to marketing success is eliminated.

Product sampling has become one of the hottest consumer sales promotion tactics, but it is more sophisticated than simply mailing free samples. Targeted give-away programs are run with retailers, on airplanes, in theaters and hotels, through a special newspaper industry sampling program (developed originally by Gannett Newspapers) and through media-sponsored mall tours.

Product sampling has shown the most growth over the past two years of the 11 types of consumer promotions tracked by Donnelley Marketing. Sixty-four percent of companies tracked by Donnelley use sampling techniques, with 43% using sampling for established products. Showing decreased use over that period were premium promotions, sweepstakes and rebates.

Sampling is moving beyond the traditional packaged goods industry. During Spring Break in Daytona Beach, General Motors encouraged students to test drive their Geos, and MCI allowed them to call home for free.

An important opportunity for media companies is to understand how traditional electronic and print media can serve this growing business for marketers. With interactive capabilities, whether telephone or electronic, television offers marketers the ability to generate specific viewer requests for items. Costs are often prohibitive, suggesting that media will create special sampling packages. Turner Broadcasting has developed several concepts to enable sponsors of their various media services with the opportunity to participate in special sampling programs. Arts & Entertainment Network, through their A&E Viewers Club, is exploring ways to allow marketers to include special samples in quarterly member mailings.

Magazines are repackaging their publications in special wrappers to enable advertisers to include free product samples. Both electronic and print media are offering viewers and readers free incentives and offers from selected advertisers, ranging from packaged goods products to hotels, airlines, financial services and fast-food outlets.

One of the great untapped resources existing for traditional media is their ability to deliver consumer promotion capabilities to their advertisers. Whether they are within the pages of magazines or wrapped with them, distributed via mail to loyal viewers of television programs and networks, or given away at media-sponsored mall tours, free samples and coupons provide an appealing means to enhance the value and increase the accountability of traditional media.

⚲

THE MOST ROMANTIC MEDIUM

One of the great phenomena of media today is the romance novel. Steamy romance novels account for 46% of all mass marketed paperback books sold in the United States. Spending on the romance market rose to an estimated $750 million in 1991, including books and romance magazines. Waldenbooks, with 1,100 stores, reports that romance sales were up 27% in 1991 and 35% in 1992. Total book sales are up less than 5%.

Amazingly, fully 60% of U.S. households did not buy a single book last year, but the average romance novel customer spent $1,200, according to book retailer Barnes & Noble. That averages 240 paperbooks at $4.99 apiece. According to Harlequin, the leading romance novel publisher, over half its customers buy an average of 30 novels a month!

Romance readers tend to be women, average age 39 years. Forty-five percent are college educated and more than 50% are working, with an average household income of $40,000. One interesting statistic: according to a 1985 *Psychology Today* article, "women who read romance novels make love to their partners 74% more often than do nonreaders."

Romance novel readers have their own convention, magazine (*Romantic Times*), special cruises, 900# services, and their own pin-up star! Fabio Lanzoni modeled for more than 100 romance novels last year. His piercing blue eyes and flowing blond hair help assure strong sales for the books he graces.

Fabio has his own 900# which, at $1.99 per minute, brought in $25,000 from 8,000 calls in its first two months, according to *Forbes* Magazine. Fabio has his own T shirts, has written his own book, published by Avon, and is on tap to star in an action-adventure-*romance* movie.

This booming genre is an untapped goldmine for potential sponsors. Advertisers have been reluctant to support romance in print, although they have made television soap operas one of the medium's most consistently profitable areas. K-III Magazines' *Soap Opera Digest* and *Soap Opera Weekly,* while successful at the newsstand, have met with lukewarm support from the advertising community.

Yet these vehicles offer advertisers strong audience loyalty, reader involvement, a clearly defined editorial focus, and a franchise opportunity. In the 1990s, we can expect several marketers to embrace the soap opera and romance genre, become visible sponsors of the magazines, books, conventions, cruises, *and* the stars. *Romance Classics,* a new cable network created by *American Movie Classics'* parent Rainbow Program Holdings, is totally commercial-free. But Rainbow may be receptive to mutually advantageous relationships with marketers.

Romance is just one of the growing grassroots growth businesses that offer tremendous marketing opportunities in the 1990s. When large groups of people share a common interest, and no traditional marketer has locked into a sponsorship position, opportunities exist.

STAR TREK, BASEBALL CARDS AND '50s TELEVISION

Drive down your local Main Street. What store is there today that was not there two years ago? More than likely, it's the sports memorabilia store, trading on the tremendous popularity in sports trading cards and other memorabilia. If you haven't walked in, do it today. The market for cards, figures, posters, autographs and other related paraphernalia is enormous. Not a weekend passes without a local hotel hosting a card trading show. Teams are now hosting their own major shows, with stars from today and yesterday signing autographs for $5 to $35 each.

The amazing thing about these stores, exhibitions and products is that they are unsponsored. It's the same for the *Star Trek* conventions that attract thousands of fans from around the world. Why have marketers not discovered these opportunities to relate to a highly targeted, well-defined audience? Why hasn't a major company become the name sponsor for the major *Star Trek* conventions, or the big sports card trading shows? We can be certain they will. Not only is this an opportunity for marketers, but for fans as well. It will help reduce admission costs, assure better produced shows, and attract larger crowds.

Nick-at-Nite network has demonstrated the growing interest in television from the 1950s and 1960s as a collectible opportunity. Early television is becoming a grassroots phenomenon, appreciated worldwide. Not only can advertisers associate themselves more strongly with N-A-N, but they can create and sponsor conventions, traveling exhibits, promotional tie-ins, etc.

Recently, I was talking to a top entertainment attorney about the continuing interest in 1950s and 1960s television programs. We realized that *Nick-at-Nite* is just the beginning of a phenomenon. During the next several years, we concluded, major networks and syndicators will produce *new* episodes of classics such as *Have Gun, Will Travel* (which was the first TV program written by *Star Trek* creator Gene Roddenberry), *The Six Million Dollar Man, Route 66* and *Gunsmoke.* CBS has dominated the ratings when they air classic episodes of *Mary Tyler Moore, All In The Family, Carol Burnett* and *The Ed Sullivan Show. Jeopardy* returned from oblivion to become the second highest rated program in syndication. Fourth run episodes of *Columbo* still manage to win their time period whenever they air.

Certain classics have retained name brand equity and high awareness. Still loyal viewers will sample these programs based on name alone -- and are likely to stay if their expectations are fulfilled. The challenge is a creative one, but no less a creative challenge exists for each and every new television program. And no less a challenge existed for the Broadway producers who have successfully revived *Guys & Dolls* and many other classic Broadway hits. *Maverick, The Fugitive, Dennis the Menace,* and *The Beverly Hillbillies* are all being made into movies, following the success of *Dragnet, Star Trek* and *The Untouchables.* Television programmers should not allow valued properties, in which there is a great deal of equity, to be lost to other media.

Intelligent marketers will be well served by anticipating network television and syndication revivals of classic programs and linking with them for promotional and marketing programs.

§

146

LOTTERIES, SWEEPSTAKES, COUPONS, FREEBIES

While marketers use promotions, coupons and free samples to help move product and create awareness, they have yet to recognize that consumers are fascinated by them. The very existence and growth of these industries offers marketers several new opportunities.

Magazines now serve those who are most interested in these vehicles. Consumers pay for subscriptions to *Freebies* Magazine and *Lottery, Contest* and *Sweepstakes* newsletters. They are growth industries. Not only can marketers distribute sweepstakes, samples and coupons through these publications, but they can communicate highly targeted advertising messages directly to audiences that are most likely to respond.

Local communities have coupon trading clubs, where consumers in their 50s trade Pampers coupons to "Twentysomethings" in return for ExLax coupons. Will a television program or interactive computer coupon trading club be developed soon? Probably. Should marketers be aware of the program to promote their own couponing efforts? Definitely.

Lotteries are becoming more widespread and there have been some examples of promotional tie-in activity. States offer marketers the opportunity to gain an extraordinary in-store presence through lottery re-sellers, and can convert each losing lottery ticket into a coupon. 7-Eleven Stores have done this on their own, offering special discounts with a losing lottery ticket.

THE SCHOOLS AS BATTLEGROUND

Whittle Communications' *Channel One* and the cable industry's *Cable in the Classroom* have invested millions of dollars to place satellite dishes, cable hook-ups, video recorders and large screen televisions in more than 15,000 high schools serving nearly 16 million high school students.

Chris Whittle, chairman of Whittle Communications, is the point person in the growing battle between print-based and electronic education. The educational system in this country is founded on dependence upon and commitment to the printed words. Books are the primary resource for educating our children. Yet, as pointed out in a previous chapter, 60% of U.S. households don't even purchase books for pleasure reading. Twenty-five percent of all Americans aged 19-23 have not completed high school.

There is a dynamic conflict between students, who are a part of an electronic generation, and educators who are committed to the culture of the printed word. There are some people in this country who believe that the concept of television in the schools subverts the educational process, and that the idea of advertising support for this television programming is downright catastrophic. From California to New York, these educators are fighting a losing battle against the tides of the future.

Is it reasonable to think that young people who have been exposed to more than one-half million television commercials in their lifetime can be unreasonably influenced by seeing another message in their school? It certainly supports Whittle's sales presentation to advertisers if educators believe these messages are in such a powerful environment that they will overwhelm any other commercial exposure students may receive.

Is the school such a sacrosanct place that it must be pure from any commercial activity? Advertising supported publications have always been provided in schools. As a child, I remember touring the Borden Dairy facility in our town and as a high school student touring the Utica Club Beer facility. General Electric, which manufactured radios in Utica, used the high schools as focus group facilities. I remember when we shocked the General Electric moderator when every participant in the group voted for the tiniest transistor radio over the larger portable models. Was this a commercial activity that would be unacceptable by today's standards? We students gained as much from these companies' efforts as they did -- perhaps more.

Educators have no argument with Mind Extension University, an advertising supported venture funded by Denver-based Jones Intercable. ME/U brings classroom programming into the home, allowing those who did not complete their education to receive accredited high school and college diplomas via advertising supported television. Is it so radically inappropriate for students in the school to receive 12 minutes of valuable television programming daily with four minutes of advertising?

As Whittle launches his Edison Project to create lower cost private schools throughout the country, he is taking on the educational community directly. He can expect opposition to mount from this community, targeted directly at his funding resource -- advertisers on Channel One.

The choice we have in this country is for our educational system to join the electronic age and communicate to students in ways they can understand and to which they can relate. Or our schools can continue to use outmoded forms of communications and become the daytime prisons for millions of young people, as they have become in our inner cities.

I am not advocating a total conversion to electronics; certainly schools are the place where young people should learn to love reading. But schools cannot afford to exclude electronic communications. And they cannot afford the costs of equipment and programming. The educational system should be grateful to Chris Whittle and to marketers who have agreed to fund his vision through advertising support.

Marketers, through Channel One programming, have the opportunity to assure that students become involved with the political process. They are being given the responsibility for assuring that students witness the events taking place around the world that are shaping their future. Marketers can support AIDS education, anti-drug messages and environmental training in a format and style with which students can be involved and from which they can learn. Why should a handful of educators refuse support from the private sector? The answer can only be fear and jealousy.

Marketers have played the most important role in assuring America's freedoms throughout the last century. The support of advertising revenues built the newspaper, magazines, and television industries. Without it, CNN could not exist. It supported the success of the American Olympics teams in Albertville and Barcelona. It underwrites public television and helps to gain recognition for basic human rights through the portrayal of minorities in programming, through international news coverage and public service advertising campaigns.

As the marketing community defines its support for Channel One, the battlelines should be clearly recognized. The decision to support or not support Channel One cannot be simply a numbers issue of cost efficiencies or be influenced by small thinking activist group pressures. Marketers have an obligation to support our nation's students and schools and to assure the effectiveness of our educational system.

EVERYWHERE YOU GO, I'LL BE WATCHING YOU

The recent rise of "place-based" and "in-store" media is not a fad. The challenge, however, is for the many companies fighting for a niche in this emerging media arena to prove that in-store and place-based media succeed in breaking through the noise level of advertising messages and generate sales results.

Are consumers receptive to greater in-store activity? Coupons are distributed in the aisles and at check-out. Television sets are dropping down from ceilings throughout the store and swinging into customers' faces as they wait at the check-out line. Radio blares down messages of special sales and promotions.

Turner Broadcasting, although it is not proceeding with the Checkout Channel in supermarkets, continues to explore the Airport Channel and the McDonald's Network. Out-of-home opportunities are being developed for bars and restaurants, 7-Eleven convenience stores and other national chains, golf and health clubs, movie theaters, phone booths, shopping malls, ski resorts and stores, stadiums and arenas, and truck stops.

Are in-store media viewed as traditional media? Or are they considered to be consumer promotion? Some suggest that they are a cross between both. Are placed-based media a further scourge on the landscape, or are they a legitimate effort to communicate with a population that is more mobile than ever and has less leisure time than ever before?

The growth of place-based and in-store media reflect the growing concern among marketers with the increasing fragmentation of traditional media, and recognition that the closer they can get to the actual point-of-purchase, the more likely they are to influence that purchase decision. Place-based media will take many shapes and forms during the next several years. As with any new media form, the key issue will be how effectively they are able to gain distribution and then prove to advertisers that they, in fact, can achieve specific marketing objectives.

Place-based media companies will be dependent upon the research industry's ability to develop meaningful measures of performance and the marketing community's willingness to accept new standards rather than insisting on comparisons to traditional media.

RETAILER SOLICITATION PROGRAMS

As outlined previously, a major early cause of the shift toward trade allowances was the development by retailers of "vendor solicitation programs" in cooperation with media companies. A similar opportunity exists today to construct cooperative programs between manufacturers and media companies to solicit retail funds.

The scenario is relatively simple. Representatives of several media companies, either consultants or ad agencies, organize a group of non-competitive products to agree to fund a major advertising campaign promoting a specific consumer promotional "event." The event might be a campaign promoting summer barbecues, or a special Thanksgiving focus, or even as simple as a "Pasta Week" promotion. The manufacturers agree to fund extensive activity to build consumer awareness of this event, including in-store displays, in-store cents-off reductions, a free standing coupon insert supporting the event, sweepstakes, plus heavy advertising promoting the brands included in the event. The advertising and promotional efforts of the participating brands will have their own focus as well as maintaining an umbrella theme.

This virtually duplicates one of the successful approaches taken by retailers in their early vendor support programs. The difference is that manufacturers will promote and support only those retailers who agree to fund the program with dollars deducted from current trade and slotting allowances. The advertising and promotion will directly name those participating chains where the promotion can be found, contest entered, etc. To conform to governmental Robinson-Patman Act regulations, the program must be made equally available to all retailers who purchase the products, but the same realities that enabled the retailer to slip through special arrangements exist today for the manufacturers who must now balance the scales.

This approach is a simplification of a very complex effort. The reality is that the first beneficiaries of the effort will be local media and consumer promotion companies; but the important goal is to shift retail trade support dollars back into media and to reverse the tide of budgets which now is flowing away from traditional media and promotion. The key components are that several media and promotion companies must cooperate and multiple manufacturers must be involved. For the entrepreneurial advertising company, this concept represents an important opportunity. In the 1970s, several new companies formed for the sole purpose of working with retailers and media companies to create vendor solicitation programs. A similar opportunity exists today, but the industry would be better served if ad agencies could provide the impetus and service.

A GOAT FOR A FENCE

There was a time when barter deals were simple. A guy with a couple of extra goats would need a fence built, so he'd give one of the goats to a tradesman in exchange for building a fence.

Today, the *perception* of barter is that it is much more complicated than exchanging goats for labor, but that is something of a misperception, according to those in the barter media business (defined as exchanging products or services for media time, as opposed to barter syndication, which is the exchange of television programming to stations in return for control of advertising time).

The International Reciprocal Trade Association says $2.6 billion in media time and space was placed through barter media deals in 1991, up from $1.6 billion in 1986 and $1.0 billion in 1981. This spectacular growth has been fueled by a combination of economic realities and a better understanding among advertisers of how to make barter deals work for them.

Alan Elkin, CEO of Active Media Services, Inc., says advertisers are recognizing that barter media offers a "great alternative for liquidating product." A typical barter deal would start with an advertiser possessing a large inventory of surplus merchandise, which is given at wholesale value to media barter companies in return for media time that is typically marked up. Usually, some cash also changes hands.

In tough economic times when surplus merchandise and excess media supply are available, barter is especially appealing to both marketers and media. John Kramer, president of Media Store Inc., advises that individual media barter firms tend to excel in particular media, and that marketers must be careful to match the barter company with the media required to implement their marketing plan. He also suggests that the value of the media received be carefully evaluated to assure fair value for the merchandise supplied.

We can expect that media barter will become a more respected weapon in the marketer's arsenal as media supply continues to grow and as companies, such as Turner Broadcasting System, expand their own in-house barter operations. The expansion of global media and marketing also creates significant new barter opportunities.

ETHNIC MEDIA -- COMMITMENT OR PANDERING?

Ethnic media are the fastest growing traditional media arenas. Inherent to their success is the receptivity of marketers to developing products and advertising targeted to these audiences. While marketers have demonstrated an eagerness to focus on these audiences, activist groups (See Part One) have often criticized them for doing so.

Media opportunities exist to reach virtually every major, and several minor, ethnic groups in the United States. Marketers are faced with the challenge of determining how aggressively they can support these media. On one hand, ethnic media are charged with further eroding the American "melting pot" ideal. Individual ethnic groups, they charge, should not be encouraged to maintain their native language and unique identity, but should be integrated into society. When maintaining natural ethnic differences translates into segregated education and societal separation, their argument takes on added relevance.

Others argue against ethnic differentiation from a different point of view. They claim that marketing efforts targeted toward ethnic groups smacks of pandering and takes advantage of specific ethnic characteristics for commercial gain. This issue is particularly evident in the alcohol and tobacco products categories.

But criticism leveled at these companies for developing products targeted to ethnic audiences increases the risks for other marketers and their fears that they will be equally criticized.

The fastest growing segment of U.S. population is the Hispanic market. Hispanics represent 9% of total U.S. population, but this group is growing at a rate of 34% a year, compared to 7% for the general population. A major report issue by ad agency DMB&B reports that the purchasing power of Hispanics almost tripled from $59 million to $165 million in the past ten years. From 1984 to 1990 advertisers more than doubled their spending in Hispanic media from $285 million to $628 million. In the last decade the percentage of Hispanics who are college educated has grown 21% and the percentage of Hispanics with household incomes over $50,000 has increased 26% (in real dollars).

According to the DMB&B report, Strategy Research Corporation has segmented the Hispanic population into three groups it calls Relatively Unassimilated (40.1%), Partially Assimilated (45.0%) and Highly Assimilated (14.9%). A.C. Nielsen has created three similar segments it calls Spanish Language Dominant (51.3%), Bilingual (25.4%) and English Dominant (23.3%).

Based on these statistics, it is apparent that marketers seeking to influence this fast-growing segment of the population must be cognizant of language issues. But equally important are cultural differences.

A major issue for marketers to recognize is that Hispanics, Afro-Americans, Asians and Gays (although they are not an ethnic group) are not seeking to assimilate into society in the same ways that Jews, Italians, Irish and earlier ethnic groups sought to place their Americanism ahead of their heritage.

Instead, groups are reinforcing their ethnicity, and the media choices they make reflect their cultural standards. Society must adapt to these realities. The efforts of Afro-Americans, Hispanics, Gays or any other heterogeneous segment of society to maintain and promote their unique cultural differences are a strength of our country and must be recognized as such. Marketers must be responsive to these realities. They must, of course, be sensitive to issues of health and welfare. But if it is not inappropriate for Virginia Slims to target a female smoker, why, then, is it inappropriate to develop a marketing campaign for a cigarette targeted to Afro-Americans?

During the 1990s and beyond, we can expect marketers to aggressively develop products and marketing programs targeted toward ethnic audiences. Philip Morris recently developed marketing campaigns specifically targeted to the Gay community, which were well received by both Gays and Gay media.

In the 1970s and 1980s marketers were criticized for not developing products specifically designed for ethnic minorities and for not incorporating a sufficient number of minorities in their advertising. In the 1990s, government and public pressure groups are forcing marketers to withdraw products that are specifically intended to serve the needs, interests and desires of particular ethnic groups, accusing advertising executives of pandering to minorities.

Television's most popular personalities include Bill Cosby, Oprah Winfrey and Arsenio Hall; the cable industry has given voice to networks and programs targeted to Black, Hispanic, Japanese, Chinese, Greek and other ethnic groups. Advertising has been a primary contributor to the success and popularity of Bo Jackson, Magic Johnson and Michael Jordan; marketers are aggressively taking a leadership role in responding to the nation's increased awareness of and attention to ethnic diversity. While some would use these efforts to suggest intentions that are somehow subversive, most thoughtful citizens realize that advertising is the funding resource that enables ethnic groups to maintain their unique cultures.

Media targeted to ethnic audiences will continue to grow. Creative media executions intended to reach and influence these groups will also be developed. These targeted marketing and media efforts represent an important opportunity for economic growth of ethnic media. Some people suggest that such marketing and media efforts are inappropriate. By extension, they are suggesting that the basic human rights to maintain one's heritage and be proud of individual character are unacceptable in America. Censorship in any form cannot be tolerated. Protests against marketing and advertising campaigns targeted to ethnic markets, although cloaked in morality issues, reinforce the worst instincts of America and should be exposed for the bigotry they reflect.

CAUSE-RELATED MARKETING

Environmental marketing claims are regulated so extensively by states and the federal government that the public good has suffered. Advertising is the most effective means to create public awareness and support for important issues. For several years, marketers have been at the regulatory whim of federal and state enforcement agencies that often acted inconsistently, impeding marketers' ability to develop national environmental marketing programs. When, in late 1992, the Federal Trade Commission finally stepped in and issued a set of standard guidelines, it served to "jump-start" environmental marketing, according to Juanita Duggan, Senior VP-Government Affairs for the National Food Processors Association. Environmental marketing efforts had waned due to enforcement actions of several state attorney generals and legislatures.

"In 1988-89, we started to hear about green marketing after a Roper Poll said people were willing to pay a premium for environmentally better products," Ms. Duggan stated in a *Advertising Age* interview. "But national manufacturers were not going to comply with six different sets of rules...because of the cost...so they removed those claims until the FTC moved." Not only were they restricted by inconsistent rules, but even if they attempted to conform with rules, marketers were faced with constant threats of new rules and rule changes. Without the ability to market environmentally sound products and charge a premium to consumers for their efforts, these programs and environmental enhancements stalled.

Over-regulation resulted in nearly five years of hesitation by marketers eager to expand their efforts to market more environmentally sound products. While marketers accept the need for regulation, they require consistency and conformity to develop meaningful national marketing programs that inform and motivate consumers to support their efforts. The result has been an actual decline in consumer interest in environmental marketing since 1989. Now, with the FTC taking action and requesting state regulators to conform to FTC guidelines, marketers finally can promote the environmental attributes of their products.

Green marketing is just one example of the opportunities that will be reinvented in the 1990s as corporations and consumers understand the importance of communications for establishing public awareness and reinforcing corporate commitment to causes that are in the public interest. Corporations will associate their marketing efforts with education, the homeless, human rights, AIDS and other major diseases, international affairs and other cause-related programs.

REGIONAL AND LOCAL MEDIA

Arnie Semsky, Media Director for BBDO, likes to quote the BBDO strategy of "thinking global, acting local." Andrew Orgel, former president of cable network The Box, thinks that marketers will be targeting "right to the individual." Research services such as Claritas' Prizm provide marketers with well-defined, almost block-by-block, targeting capabilities.

Realistically, marketing tactics are being created to respond to regional consumer differences. National marketers have realized that their strongest competitors are often those with highly localized pockets of loyalty who can concentrate their marketing budgets against these narrow groups. As marketers have extended their brand franchise area to amortize marketing and manufacturing costs, others have taken advantage of regional consumer tastes and preferences to develop unique products. Grits sell well in the South and offer strong competition to hot cereal products that are dominant in other parts of the country. Coors was a dominant regional brand in the West, but has had success in extending its franchise nationally. These different realities both reflect the confused marketing picture existing today.

National brands with national marketing campaigns are subject to competition from highly localized brands. Conversely, brands that are too localized may not have the resources or profitability to grow their businesses. One of the primary solutions in keeping with the "think global, act local" concept is regional distribution of national media.

Ideally, regional distribution provides marketers with the cost efficiencies of national media, the regionalization of advertising messages, and the ability to "heavy up" advertising in certain regions.

One of the quiet areas of growth in the network television business during the past several years has been the increased demand for regional network coverage. Broadcast networks have the capabilities to marry regional advertisers together, enabling different advertisers to "own" the same commercial unit in different regions of the country. Through this same capability, marketers can distribute different regional commercials according to distinctive regional marketing needs. Currently, networks do not aggressively promote this capability, but marketers are using the service with increased frequency.

Magazines have offered regional distribution capabilities for more than two decades, but the systems have become more sophisticated, allowing marketers to gain greater control over both circulation and messages. In *1981*, Jim Walsh, then advertising manager of Merrill Lynch, commented:

"My personal pet peeve is demographic and geographic editions -- those wonderful magazine segments that reach only part of the total circulation that the advertiser wants to reach. They sound like perfect marketing tools. The trouble is they don't work very well. Like many advertisers, Merrill Lynch pays a handsome premium to target its message to these more qualified readers. And like everyone else, we often end up in the back of the book, 'banked' into six or eight pages of ads."

"The explanations for 'banking' are weak and unsatisfactory. In this day of computerized printing presses it should be possible to eliminate or at least reduce the problem."

Publishers today tell us that, more than 12 years later, the problems can be eliminated, but have yet to be totally resolved. Not all magazines are printed on computerized presses. Advertisers still have not expressed a willingness to pay the significantly increased rates required for full incorporation of "split" circulation advertising runs.

Publishers further point out that regional and demographic "banks" are integrated into different positions within the publication, but those advertisers who have purchased the full circulation run have earned the right to the best positions. Even if advertisers are paying a premium for targeted circulation, it is still less than the costs full-run advertisers are paying. They also suggest that, since 1981, the magazine industry itself has become far more segmented, enabling advertisers to target almost as narrowly as they want. Each magazine values its full circulation as a whole and urges advertisers to purchase it as such.

With the improvement of direct marketing information and increased emphasis on regional marketing, advertisers will continue to pressure for improved distribution and printing procedures to even further enhance the magazine industry's targeting capabilities.

GLOBAL MEDIA AND MARKETING

Although this book focuses on the marketing business in the United States, we cannot lose sight of the reality that the same issues are equally relevant on a global scale. Ted Levitt, Professor of Marketing at Harvard suggests that "companies must learn to operate as if the world were one large market -- ignoring superficial regional and national differences." In the 1980s, we witnessed the expansion of major British, French, German and Japanese businesses taking dominant positions in the American marketing, advertising, media and entertainment industries.

Advertising agencies are measured today by the extent of their worldwide network and the global marketing capabilities they offer. Marketers are intrigued by the newly opened markets and growth opportunities offered around the world. Media companies are forming joint ventures to expand cable and satellite distribution in other nations. MTV and CNN both offer a single worldwide media buy, which Coca-Cola became the first company to take advantage of in 1992.

Although actions may become increasingly local, we cannot help but "think global." As we consider the importance of U.S.-based marketers, advertising agencies and media companies, their contribution to the economic viability of a free economy becomes even more critical to the emerging economies in Eastern Europe and the former Soviet Bloc.

The international marketplace is important not only for distribution of American products, but also for the creation of television programming. Michael Garin, senior managing director of Furman, Selz believes:

"Globalization is really driven by a couple of factors.

Number one is the change in the United States that has made deficits greater and forced people to look at the international value of their products to make up for the deficit. Secondly, the changes that have gone on overseas, at the same time, which have enhanced those values; namely the privatization of broadcasting and the same kinds of technological changes, cable, home video, and DBS, which have created new markets and competition for product."

Sidney Sheinberg, President of MCA (which is owned by Japanese electronics giant Matsushita) was quoted in *Electronic Media*:
"The reality is we can't go back to the way things were. We're entering the 21st century, and we'd better be prepared to move into that future in some way that is compatible with the new requirements of the marketplace."

The reality is that no strategy, no new look at the market, no business analysis, no evaluation of opportunities can be complete without an understanding of the global implications. The international marketplace represents the most important source of partnership opportunities, co-funding ventures and coproduction efforts.

John M. Eger, endowed professor of communications at San Diego State University and former President of CBS International, stated:
"As [global corporations] begin unfolding global media strategies, I believe we will see a steady convergence of economics, technology and public policy likely to result in the development of truly global networks, truly global integrated systems of information and communications. Our technology is

providing the means for a vast flow of information, data and new ideas throughout the world.... The world is bound together by an electronic nerve system carrying news, money, data and information almost anywhere in the world in microseconds. The fact is the influence of global media, the demand for global markets and the pressure for national solutions to essentially global problems are changing the role -- indeed, some would say the existence -- of the nation state, changing the conduct of foreign policy and compelling a rethinking of existing institutions, structures and relationships."

In many countries where industries are just being developed, management is less burdened with baggage of the past -- structures and systems that are outmoded and restrictive. Executives are identifying those business opportunities and management techniques that will enable them to compete most effectively. In the future, international companies will elevate competition to an even more intense level. The opportunity exists to embrace international marketers as partners rather than competitors, and to be open to the internationalization of business on every front. As John Eger points out, "Yes, it's a brave new world, a world where new alliances are made and old ones changed or altered dramatically."

The marketing, advertising and media businesses are global pipelines for ideas and products. The changes that take place in the United States immediately impact on decisions made in Europe, Japan, Central and South America, Canada, Great Britain and Asia. We are, in all ways, the global village that Marshall McLuhan promised.

REALITY OR HOT AIR?

The concepts that I've identified in Part 3 are not necessarily new. Some have been used by selected advertisers and in selected ways by media companies. The major change for the future is that the emphasis on *impact, exclusivity, dominance* and *frequency* will become the norm rather than the exception. Accountability is the watchword of the advertising industry; those responsible for developing media and marketing strategies will be equally responsible for validating their effectiveness.

Those marketers, agencies and media companies that are prepared for changes in the basic operating and reporting structures of their businesses, that most aggressively pursue change and adjust to new business demands are those who will win the battle for growth and success in the 1990s and into the new millenium.

!
◆

PART 4

THE FUTURE IS NOW:

MARKETING, ADVERTISING AGENCIES
AND MEDIA STRUGGLE TO GROW

CAN THE AD BUSINESS BE SAVED
FROM THE PROMOTIONAL PURGE?

Spending in traditional advertising media will invariably continue to erode unless the advertising industry significantly refocuses its energies, resources and attention. There are solutions. Ad agencies and media companies, before they can begin to address the serious problems they face, must restructure their organizations to focus on their *capabilities* and how they can best improve advertisers' sales results. Effectiveness must become the watchword of the industry, with all research and marketing efforts targeted toward clearly demonstrating how advertising motivates the consumer and contributes to each marketer's specific objectives.

Media must learn to work with each other; agencies and marketers must end the incessant scourge of commoditized pricing to encourage media to provide the resources necessary to prove their value. Agencies must create a new level of management -- the Knowledge Resources Manager – to pull all the marketing resources under a single umbrella fully focused on identifying their clients' needs and achieving their goals.

Success in the 1990s and beyond requires an understanding of new marketing dynamics and a repackaging of advertising and media organizations.

MEDIA'S CORE-VALUE

Building marketing value is a core issue for the future growth and success of traditional media. "Core value" represents the combination of media efficiency with measurable results. Advertisers and agencies have traditionally been satisfied with media measures of performance based solely upon cost efficiency of total potential audience reached, assuming the existence of effectiveness. This assumption is no longer valid. In the future, media companies must validate their effectiveness in communicating the advertisers' messages to their audiences and *also* provide cost efficiencies. Accomplishing this requires that they be capable of developing marketing programs that relate to and serve the unique objectives of each client.

The concept of marketing support has glibly been referred to as *value-added*. Value-added is, however, a more basic form of support provided to advertisers *after the fact* of their making a commitment to purchase time or space in a medium. Value-added encompasses tickets, hospitality merchandising, special promotions, "billboards" (those special 'brought-to-you-by' mentions) or advantageous positioning.

While value-added offers are important tools for buyers and sellers and serve to enhance the value of a media buy, they are no more than a band-aid on an open wound. As budgets continue to bleed into promotional activities, the media industry must focus on major efforts to stop the flow and heal the wound.

This requires building strong marketing relationships with both agencies and advertisers, and providing improved understanding of how each medium works and *how* media can best contribute to achieving specific marketing objectives.

Media companies will become more involved with the "trade," the retail stores and distributors who control the flow of product to end consumers. Similarly, media companies will require direct input from their advertisers' marketing and sales executives, in order to better understand their sales and purchase dynamics. The goal of marketers is to sell their products or services to consumers. The goal of advertising is, ultimately, to have an impact on consumers' motivations. The goal of media is to communicate advertising messages and motivate the audience. Inevitably, these three hands must link with a common understanding of goals and objectives. Industry dynamics that have forced these hands apart like a magnet's opposite poles are being dramatically reversed and will, just as inevitably, create a mutual attraction.

In this section, I explain the industry dynamics that are making this shift possible.

RETAIL POWER AND THE FUTURE OF MARKETING

The crucial battleground for marketers these days is inside the stores, not in the media. Bar-code scanners are used in the majority of supermarkets in America, providing retailers with a great deal of knowledge about product sales and the effectiveness of different promotional activities. Manufacturers once held the cards, controlling promotions and dictating to retailers the prices and space needs of their products. Today, those roles have been reversed. Retailers can value each cubic inch of their shelf space and dictate to manufacturers how much profit their products must return to occupy particular space.

According to Nielsen Marketing Research, major packaged goods manufacturers spent $36 billion on trade promotion in 1991, twice what they spent on advertising. As the share of budgets committed to consumer and trade promotion increased throughout the 1980s, media companies ignored this competition. Now, however, promotion has become such a dominant force that it no longer can be ignored. The question is whether media should attack promotion or seek new ways to ally itself and find common cause.

Sales promotion and trade promotion are two separate and distinct activities. Sales promotion is manufacturer controlled, while trade promotion defines shelf space slotting allowances and other payments directly to or in support of retailers and distributors. Within each area, there is a role and opportunity for media.

In 1992, Procter & Gamble and, to a lesser extent, Kraft General Foods took up arms against retailers' stranglehold on marketing dollars. P&G launched an "every day low prices" strategy, promising to minimize retailers' control over pricing strategies. P&G lowered prices on 40% of its U.S. products and cut its $1.6 billion trade allowance budget. P&G Chairman Ed Artzt vowed to pass on savings to customers while gaining their loyalty through increased advertising. KGF followed by cutting back on their promotion budget in a limited number of product categories and cutting prices accordingly. The goal of these efforts is to restore the balance of power between marketer and retailer.

The real drama in this effort is how much support other manufacturers will give to the P&G effort. Will they follow P&G's lead with similar e-d-l-p programs? P&G and KGF are the dominant food services manufacturers and cannot be compared to other companies. They have far more flexibility in their ability to maneuver within the retail community. They can cut back on trade allowances, but simultaneously be very aggressive in their sales promotion activities and support of various sales programs, working with individual retailers.

But without support from other manufacturers, retailers may continue to have the upper hand. P&G claims it will phase out all deep discounts and offer the same price every day to retailers and wholesalers in an effort to eliminate high cost promotions, and reduce retailers' ability to stockpile products purchased at discount prices and sell them at normal prices to consumers after the promotional period. The natural instinct of retailers will be to give shelf space to those products returning more profits to their bottom-line. P&G hopes to reshape the supermarket pricing system and wean consumers off promotions and coupons by accustoming them to every-day pricing.

The program either will increase P&G's power and control by overhauling the way retailers conduct business -- or damage P&G's market share and force it back into aggressive promotional activity. Many retailers and wholesalers initially reacted by pruning back on their P&G orders, eliminating marginal P&G brands from their shelves, adding surcharges to some P&G products to compensate for lost profits, and moving P&G products to less visible shelf space. P&G, in turn, announced that it was eliminating marginal brands. Major retailers Kmart and Wal-mart support every-day-low-pricing because, among other reasons, it assures a constant flow of products into and out of warehouses. Other major retailers appear to be falling in line behind e-d-l-p.

P&G helped create the promotional bandwagon onto which retailers jumped throughout the 1980s. P&G and other manufacturers relied upon trade promotions to build short-term market share and to introduce myriad new products and line extensions. Retailers and wholesalers learned to wait for promotional periods to make the bulk of their purchases. According to trade sources, these practices generate an estimated 40% of a retailer's profits and 70% of wholesalers'.

Under the new system, the consumer would pay less than they have paid even during aggressive promotional periods, and they would pay these lower prices all year. While coupons and promotions haven't been eliminated, they have been reduced. But retailers and wholesalers are up-in-arms, seeking alternatives that will maintain their profits while continuing to satisfy consumers. Retailers' profit margins are historically low, only about one percent, not allowing them a great deal of flexibility in restructuring historic purchasing patterns.

Many in the packaged goods and retailing industries cheer P&G for taking a leadership position and making a preemptive strike to avoid America's packaged goods industry going the way of airlines, autos and other industries that haven't changed to grow. But competitive manufacturers cannot be depended upon to do what may be in their best long-term interests. A danger for P&G, said former P&G executive Frank Blod in an *Adweek* interview, is that competitors may move in with a promotional blitz to win more shelf space and gain more in-store merchandising support from retailers. In fact, H.J. Heinz has aggressively upped their promotional efforts in the past two years, slashing their advertising budgets and dramatically increasing their trade and consumer promotional spending.

In 1991, several major manufacturers decreased their ad spending, mostly attributing the decreases to poor economic conditions. Yet, even during the recessionary times, spending on trade promotions by packaged good manufacturers continued to climb, from $32 billion in 1989 to $36 billion in 1991. Traditional media advertising declined during this same period from $19 billion to $18 billion. Overall spending grew from $65 to $72 billion, with the remainder represented by consumer promotion.

Inevitably, retailers will continue to have the upper hand in the retail/manufacturer relationship because they have the relationship with the consumer. Scanner devices, when combined with "smart cards" or even "dumb" traditional credit cards, enable retailers to track purchases by customer. The next logical step is direct mail and other targeted marketing activities that can be conducted on behalf of specific marketers.

Even today, when customers buy a bottle of Coca-Cola, they can instantly be handed a coupon inviting them to purchase Pepsi for .50 cents off on their next visit. Soon, supermarket retailers will have the sophistication that retailers like Saks Fifth Avenue have depended upon for years - techniques enabling them to track their best customers' purchases and conduct marketing programs specifically targeted to individuals. Marketers will find these capabilities highly appealing. Basic marketing, which suggests that you define your best customers and potential customers, identify their needs, and then communicate with them in as effective a way as possible, inevitably moves marketing dollars to those resources that can best accomplish these goals.

The concept of trade promotion dollars has been focused, to date, on "selling in" a product -- gaining distribution and shelf space. No matter how much shelf space a product has, customers need to be aware of the product and motivated to buy it for the product to sell. Since customers have become sensitized to "deals," coupons and other sales promotion, efforts have been used by marketers to "sell through" a product.

Advertising, ideally, helps to both sell-in and sell-through. This connection must become more clearly defined to both retailers and manufacturers before advertising budgets begin an upward climb. To attract sales promotion and trade promotion budgets back to advertising, it is necessary for advertising to demonstrate that it can, in fact, perform both the sell-in and the sell-through functions.

Today, advertising is perceived as performing a role in the marketing process separate and distinct from sales promotion and trade promotion. That function is primarily described as "brand awareness and image." Marketers are likely to assign a decreasing value to this role. If advertising today represents 25% of the marketing budget, it is fair to expect that the role of brand image, while important, will decline to 15% - 20%, on average, of total marketing budgets. The enhanced capabilities of retailers created by scanners and more sophisticated smart card and direct marketing capabilities will invariably attract more trade dollars.

Ironically, media companies actually contributed to the explosive growth of trade promotion. In the 1970s, several media companies approached various retail chains suggesting that they organize presentations to manufacturers requesting special promotional dollars to support special advertising campaigns. Aggressive television campaigns were launched by supermarket chains such as Safeway, Waldbaum's, Grand Union, and Pathmark; department store chains like Bloomingdale's, Robinson's and Marshall Field; and mass merchandisers, Target Stores and Venture Stores. Hundreds of smaller audio-visual chains, toy stores and others took media funded "vendor solicitation programs" to manufacturers. Retailers receive a set amount of cooperative advertising money from manufacturers, depending totally upon the amount of product purchased. Co-op funds normally range from .5% to 2.5% of purchases, and are the same for every retailer.

However, most manufacturers also offer special "heavy-up" market dollars for special programs that help increase sales. Retailers promising to run a television campaign mentioning the product, combined with newspaper and/or circular support, in-store promotion and aggressive pricing offers could receive special support funds from multiple manufacturers often totalling several millions of dollars each year.

From 1975 to 1985, local television stations saw a dramatic

surge in local retail business as a direct result of successful vendor programs. At WCBS-TV in New York, local retail business increased from 15% of the station's business in 1976 to nearly 30% in 1980. Marketers were reluctant to be excluded from a retailer's aggressive, coordinated campaign. Several major retailers jumped on the vendor-support program bandwagon, going to manufacturers with more sophisticated and more frequent promotions.

Governmental regulations under the Robinson-Patman Act required that manufacturers treat all retailers equally. If they supported one vendor support program in a market, it opened the Pandora's Box to others. Co-op budgets, which had been only a small component of the marketing effort, ballooned throughout the 1980s. The funds for these efforts came directly from traditional advertising. Vendor programs, which helped to grow the local television and radio business, came directly from national advertising media. Advertising was robbing Peter to pay Paul.

In addition to funding television and radio, vendor program funds were also used to fund in-store merchandising efforts, shelf space and circular distribution. In the mid-1980s, it became apparent to the retailers that they could capture the same vendor dollars without investing the money back into television and radio media. The vendor-support dollars were no longer "special"; they were institutionalized into manufacturers' sales budgets. Savvy retailers also recognized that the tremendous surge in the number of products seeking shelf-space and the manufacturers' promotional support translated into an opportunity. The vendor-support programs remained in place, but their content changed. Instead of television and newspaper support, which moved the manufacturers' monies through the retailers' pockets to others, retailers offered special incentives that kept the money in their own pockets. And they began upping the price of admission.

Retailers commanded an ever-increasing percentage of total marketing dollars in return for in-store and profitable promotional activities. Retail spending in traditional media declined. Advertising got hit on two fronts. Slotting allowances can range from a few thousand dollars to more than $100,000 per product, depending upon the retailer, the region of the country and the product. For a company to introduce a new product nationally, Nielsen reports that costs can run as high as $3 million in slotting allowances alone. On average, marketers have to spend approximately $750,000 in slotting allowances in order to gain distribution.

In addition, manufacturers will typically offer discounted prices to retailers to support cents-off offers. Retailers also charge for "facing allowances" (space on their shelves), "failure fees" (penalties if products don't achieve sales goals), and "advertising fees" (support for a store's advertising efforts). Advertising fees can support in-store advertising activity, store circulars, and traditional media. Retailers have begun allowing outside companies such as Turner Broadcasting to establish media outlets within the stores. Another company, Act Media, is one of many companies that have placed promotional services in the store, distributing coupons, samples and other forms of merchandising activity. These programs attract more promotional funds directly paid by manufacturers for which retailers are compensated. While Turner promoted the Checkout Channel as a traditional advertising medium for manufacturers, retailers value in-store media as a new revenue stream.

Indications are that retailers will remain in control of the communications and marketing process, with their enhanced capabilities further minimizing the share of manufacturers' budgets available for traditional advertising. In 1990, Don E. Schultz, professor of advertising at Northwestern's Medill School of Journalism, advised the advertising industry that the impact of scanners bodes ill for the advertising industry.

Quoted in a major *New York Times'* article on promotion, Schultz stated: "Once they start to build customer data bases, then retailers can start talking directly to those people, through direct mail or other means, and they can motivate those customers to change their shopping habits. That's potentially disastrous to national advertisers and their agencies. It's a crisis more than a transition."

While these realities apply primarily to the supermarket, comparable issues are relevant to most other major advertiser categories. Travel, financial services, entertainment, pharmaceuticals, consumer electronics, and automotive are all going through radical changes in the dynamics of their relationships with the consumer. Whether it's pricing issues, competition, dealer and distributor relationships, governmental regulations, new technologies, economic conditions or any number of other influences, business today is changing. With it, a company's ability to invest in awareness and brand image advertising is continuing to erode. Although marketing executives clearly recognize the importance of brand identity and positioning in a highly competitive environment, the influences and controls over their businesses dictate that funds be diverted to more oppor-tunistic and pressing concerns.

The most significant aspect of the P&G decision to support *every day low pricing* strategies is that it represents a fundamental examination and subsequent restructuring of P&G's methods of selling products and a redefinition of the company's efforts to directly benefit its consumers. The e-d-l-p strategy represents an effort by P&G to place consumers ahead of retailers. Every-day-low-pricing is intended to improve value for consumers. Trade promotional spending, P&G concluded, does not benefit the consumer. "There is growing public discussion of the fact that the manufacturer sees very little of its promotional dollar reach the hands of the consumer," commented Patrick L. Kiernan, an executive with the Grocery Manufacturers of America, Inc.

P&G's efforts, although risky, represent the type of change, reexamination and fundamental restructuring required by marketers, advertising agencies and media companies if advertising and media as we know them today are to survive.

Marketers' goals must be to develop resources assuring them as much direct access to the consumer and the opportunity to influence consumers' brand preferences as the retailer has available. Media has a role in this process.

ARE AD AGENCIES PREPARED TO DO BUSINESS IN THE '90S?

The demands on corporate management to deal with the dynamic conflict among trade promotion, consumer sales promotion, traditional marketing and brand equity issues create the opportunity for advertising agencies to elevate their potential role and contribution to their clients' marketing processes.

The advertising agent started as a space peddler, buying space in media wholesale, and selling it retail. Soon, when advertisers wanted something more effective to put in their ads, the peddler hired someone to plan and write them, thus taking the first step beyond being just an "agent." When more information was needed for the message, the agent went out and dug it up, making the first foray into research. Media had helped the growth of the agent by paying a commission to the agents who could represent them to advertisers and attract new business.

Soon agency services became so diverse and expensive that commissions were no longer adequate to compensate for the work provided, by now mostly performed by individuals possessed of highly developed skills.

In 1963, approximately 4,200 agencies operated in the United States, ranging from the one-man shop to world-wide organizations employing thousands. These agencies were responsible for placing approximately 40% of the $12 billion spent annually on advertising. Today, spending has grown 1,085% yet the number of agencies has grown only 21% to 5,200 agencies listed in the *Standard Directory of Advertising Agencies*. The agency *business* has been one of the most extraordinary growth industries of the past thirty years.

Agencies once presented themselves as their clients' marketing *partners,* and their compensation reflected this relationship. A 1964 college textbook on *The Advertising Agency Business* describes an advertising agency as "a highly specialized business machine for digesting an advertiser's selling problems and producing ideas for increasing his sales, his reputation, and his profits." Those ideas are not limited to the actual commercials or print ads. They encompass all components of the "machine."

Today, agencies offer several commodities that clients are viewing increasingly as *independent* services. Many advertising executives believe that it is acceptable, viable *and* appropriate to retain several agencies to perform highly specialized functions depending upon their particular skills.

They point to media buying services, which have become exceedingly profitable by offering just one capability, focusing totally on proving to clients that they provide the best and lowest cost service. Media planning and buying is recognized by many advertisers as an independent function handled in-house, through one or several agencies, or through a media buying service, or any combination of the above. The shift of media spending control away from the advertising agencies during the past 20 years has been dramatic. In 1970, agencies controlled approximately 95% of all media spending for their clients. Today, agencies control 60% - 70%, with in-house groups and media buying services capturing the difference. Western International, a Los Angeles based buying service, alone controls more than $1 billion in annual media spending. Anheuser-Busch, Bristol-Myers Squibb, Unilever, Nabisco, Chrysler and American Home Products all handle media buying, planning or both in-house.

Executives also point to the success of independent television commercial productions companies, which have enabled agencies to reduce or eliminate their own production staffs. There are independent traffic bureaus, handling the shipping of ads and commercials to media on behalf of agencies and advertisers. Many agree with Jerry Della Femina that an agency is best served by concentrating on its creative capabilities. They anticipate a reemergence of creative boutiques popular in the 1970s.

The advertising business is, by its very nature, highly competitive. Historically, the advertising industry has measured its success by total revenues. As sales promotion has eaten away at ad budgets, the advertising industry has done little to respond. Although corporations spent more on advertising, they had little knowledge of what worked and what didn't.

Agencies aggressively compete with each other for new accounts, developing speculative presentations of creative ideas -- often costing hundreds of thousands of dollars. During the past several years, advertisers have "put their accounts into review" with greater frequency, requiring their agency to "shoot it out" with others. A key element of the client's decision, especially during the past few years, has been the compensation for which the agency is willing to work. Commissions were once a standard 15%. Today, no standard exists as agency work, like media, has become a negotiable commodity. More than 50% of clients changed their compensation system between 1988 and 1992, and the majority of these companies say they did so to save money.

The decision on how to handle the media function is typically cost driven -- cost of media and/or the cost of administrative implementation. The media function is a commodity. Rarely is a choice made on a media organization because of strategic thinking and creativity issues. Rarely is a presentation made to clients on the opportunities for treating media selection and the advertising creative as a synergistic process.

Cost is a factor in client evaluations of almost every agency function and, more often than ever, it is becoming the deciding factor. Agencies now are forced to compete on an ala carte basis. Because large agencies are structured to be *service* organizations with account teams, management and extensive support costs, they usually cannot compete with specialists which provide a single capability and minimal service support. In a nutshell, competitive pressures are forcing agencies to become "sellers" of their product. To elaborate on this point, let's distinguish between the concept of "marketing" and "selling."

Marketing is the thorough understanding of a client's product, customers, needs and competition; developing with the client a set of goals and objectives; and then constructing recommendations that uniquely respond to and can measurably achieve the defined objectives.

Selling is the action of defining a product's or service's uses and offering it to a client for an agreed upon price.

Products and services that are sold rather than marketed tend to become commoditized, with pricing and profitability subject to competition and supply/demand factors. This difference between selling and marketing puts into perspective the major paradigm shift that will shatter the relationships of advertisers, agencies and media and move them in completely new directions during the next several years.

Agencies inherently understand the value and importance of positioning themselves as their clients' marketing partners. Most agency executives tell me that they truly believe they are a marketing partner to their clients. Their clients, however, disagree. Nearly 85% of advertisers report that they perceive their agencies to be "task" oriented and they compensate them accordingly. A very small minority of advertisers say their advertising agency is a full marketing partner involved in developing strategic objectives as well as solutions.

Current relationships among advertisers, advertising agencies and media are sales-based, rather than marketing-based, relationships. Although many agency executives (and media executives) would argue otherwise, those who could demonstrate the marketing foundations of their relationships are the exception to the rule. This is simply the reality of how media and advertising businesses have been most successful for the past 100 years, since the days of the first newspaper space peddler.

Advertising's primary success has been realized because demand continued to outpace supply, enabling media to continually raise prices and agencies to reap profits.

But for the 100 years, the very foundations of the way agencies and media conduct their business will be shaken to their roots by a total and permanent reversal in the supply and demand curve. If advertising agencies and media are to reverse their declining role in the communications process, they must look to the future -- not the past -- and change the definition of how they present themselves from a sales-based approach to a marketing-based strategy.

Agencies are responding. BBDO, McCann-Erickson, FCB/Leber Katz and other agencies are creating new units designed to address client needs traditionally handled by outsiders, particularly management consultants. Several agencies are testing the account planning system.

Lowe & Partners has fashioned an agency within an agency called Lowe Cable Group, a unit that specializes in advertising for cable television networks such as The Discovery Channel. Saatchi & Saatchi and DDB/Needham, along with many other major agencies, are offering media capabilities on a stand-alone basis priced to compete with media buying services. Most agencies have offered their creative department independent of other agency services. Agencies have split off their production departments into separate businesses serving other agencies and clients.

The clear trend in agencies is to place increased emphasis on their creative product and to convert agency service and support units, such as the media department, to independently profitable units. The "specialist" scenario is the most likely one for most agencies to follow in the 1990s and beyond. A powerful movement in business today, highly praised by many consultants, is breaking big business into smaller units. After years of recommending centralization to realize economies of scale, consultants now suggest that management of large centralized corporations are too removed from the marketplace and those employees who are most involved in the day-to-day workplace. Centralization, organizational experts point out, often leads to organizational chaos, as those furthest from the center become too removed from responsibility to have clear paths and directions for decision-making. The trend has become to create decentralized pockets of organization, each operating with total or near-autonomy and decision-making power.

The danger with decentralization is that corporate synergies are not comfortably accommodated. Corporate staffs given responsibility for coordinating, and even generating, multi-divisional programs are typically met with resistance, either active or passive. A corporate culture shift occurred in the late 1970s and 1980s, when many media and advertising companies underwent leveraged buyouts.

Centralized corporate financial management gained effective control of media companies and advertising agencies. This was a dramatic cultural shift for most of these companies. Media firms had traditionally been led by sales executives, and ad agencies by creative and account people. Whether centralized or decentralized, executives in most advertising and media companies were accustomed to operating with a high degree of autonomy and comparatively loose financial controls. Suddenly, executives with little experience in media or advertising, but armed with MBAs and financial training, instituted what was, in effect, an unfriendly takeover of the industry. Businesses became highly leveraged at the same time that profits began shrinking, competition became more intense, and in the late 1980s, the economy took a dramatic turn for the worse.

The initial effect for many of these companies was a reduction in manpower, followed by a total reordering of corporate priorities, leading to the elimination of complete departments. Corporations were forced to respond simultaneously to both new marketplace conditions and new internal management structures. The result was culture shock, with *internal* conflicts often preventing management from responding effectively to new *external* demands.

As marketers were struggling with their own identities, advertising agencies and media companies were increasingly self-absorbed and fighting their own internal demons to maintain profits.

The advertising business shares some surprising similarities to the medical profession. Doctors once were mostly general practitioners, highly skilled in dealing directly with patients and diagnosing their needs through an emphasis on the patients' own explanations of symptoms. The stethoscope, when it was first invented, was actually scorned by doctors because a stethoscope was associated with the lowly surgeons, who were then considered craftsmen, not doctors. Doctors were considered to have great intellect and insight. Surgeons were detached, focused on the disease or the organ, rather than on the health of the patient.

Today, we are all too familiar with the image of the doctor as a remote specialist, highly trained to perform a particular procedure, but relying for diagnosis and treatment on information from machines rather than their patients. Those operating the machines have no connection whatsoever with patients, only with blood, tissue and x-rays. Physicians no longer control the diagnostic process; nor do physicians have long-standing, personal, deep relationships with their patients.

In advertising, we can draw the same conclusions. Advertisers once considered their advertising agencies to be partners with whom they went to market. They had direct, long-standing relationships with the individuals who were most responsible for creating the advertising. Often the same person who created the ads decided on the media, placed the ads and then accompanied the client to check on the sales results.

Today, advertising is highly specialized. Account groups communicate with the client; in some corporations brand managers who have complete responsibility for a product's marketing meet with the ad agency's creative and media groups no more than once or twice each year. At several ad agencies, the media executives who are directly responsible for media planning and buying never meet their client's brand managers. Far too many advertisers perceive their relationships with advertising agencies as patients view doctors: practitioners with highly specialized skills. The agency's knowledge of its "patient" is often based upon secondary information. Relationships are increasingly tenuous and dependent upon short-term results.

The future of the advertising business depends on a renewed commitment to the diagnostic process: an in-depth understanding of marketers' goals and objectives accompanied by a total commitment to achieving those objectives.

ADVERTISING AGENCY SURVIVAL

Since 1970, the average major advertising agency has reduced personnel from ten people per million dollars in billings to 1.5 people per million. Computers and the rapid growth of ad billings are largely responsible. But at the same time that agencies have experienced staffing reductions, demands upon them have increased immensely, fueled by media fragmentation, competitive fragmentation and client transience.

To maintain its performance level, the advertising industry has developed a system of interlinked *artificial* computerized intelligence programs that support each of the various specialized services. Computers and syndicated research services allow ad agencies to build quantitative information services that complete pre-assigned informational tasks.

But computers do not compensate for the increased demands placed upon workers in advertising agencies. Peter F. Drucker points out that new technology by itself does not generate higher productivity. Computers are *tools* for providing services, dependent upon the user. Since the introduction of information technology, office and clerical forces have grown at a much faster rate than ever before. And there has been virtually no increase in the productivity of service work.

The solution for the service business suffering from increased demands and reduced manpower, suggests Drucker, is to "work smarter." The way to work smarter is to clearly define the task and the goals. However, the challenge is in the execution of this simple dogma. If the task is defined as "increasing a client's sales," the role of each department within an ad agency will become more complex and time consuming. If the task is defined by the actual function performed and how it can be accomplished more efficiently, it assures greater cost efficiency but decreased attention to the client's needs. Drucker offers the example of an insurance claims department that increased the productivity of its claims department nearly fivefold by defining its task as "paying death claims as fast and as cheaply as possible."

As a result, the company fully checks only 2% of its claims -- the largest ones -- rather than 100%. If an ad agency were to follow Drucker's advice in this example, it might define its media administration department's task as "paying media company invoices as quickly as possible" and restructure its methods to "work smarter" by examining fewer invoices. But the reality is that a large number of media invoices are, in fact, discrepant. The client has not received full value for the media investment. The agency's task is to "assure full value has been received for the client's media investment." This radically alters the Drucker formula - a task oriented philosophy focused on working smarter may, in fact, be counter productive to the actual goals of the organization.

In *Technopoly: The Surrender of Culture to Technology,* Dr. Neil Postman reminds us of Frederick Taylor's 1911 book, *Principles of Scientific Management.* Taylor's manual has been an important guideline for American business, and many of the principles that are applied to business today have their foundation in Taylor. His basic belief was that the goal of human labor and thought is efficiency. Human judgment, we should assume, cannot be trusted; subjectivity is an obstacle to clear thinking; *what cannot be measured either does not exist or is of no value.* Workers are relieved of any responsibility to think at all.

Taylor, Postman points out, holds that society is best served when human beings are placed at the disposal of their techniques and technology... that human beings are worth less than machinery. At face value, we reject this concept as absurd. Yet, too often business decisions are made on the basis of computer capabilities and financial economies. The danger is when financial management focuses on systems intended to increase productivity without clearly understanding how that decision affects clients' real needs. I don't know one agency executive who would knowingly and intentionally do a disservice to clients. But business decisions are made every day that are not responsive to the single task of achieving the client's objectives. Through this focus, agencies can clearly define the service options involved in every facet of the advertising process, and charge according to the actual cost of providing each function.

It should be the client's choice whether all invoices are thoroughly checked or whether a cross-section of the largest invoices are sampled for accuracy. A cost/benefits ratio can be established and each client can determine the value of the agency's service in each area. Agencies have been given the responsibility for the processing and administration of media contracts and invoices. As the sheer weight of responsibility has increased, compensation and manpower has declined. Advertisers and media must absorb these costs.

Some agencies provide all the services associated with advertising. Some have in-house staffs for only a few functions and use outside specialists for others. Some offer limited capabilities and leave it to the client to select other companies to provide certain capabilities. The business of advertising has become highly executional, with each component of the advertising campaign handled as a separate function. Advertising, more appropriately, should be approached as an integrated process.

The advertising agencies that are moving forward with a clear vision of the 1990s are those which view their role to be **critical thinking** *and* **the creation of knowledge about how to most effectively sell their clients' products and services.** *This shift away from the "Silver Bullet" theory (which suggests that an agency focus all its energies on the creation of the big creative idea), demands an emphasis on processes which produce knowledge and enhance critical thinking.*

IF THE RESEARCH SAYS SO, IS IT REALLY TRUE?

The greatest opportunity for media and advertising companies in the 1990s is to provide marketers with greater insight on the effectiveness of their marketing efforts in achieving specific sales goals and objectives.

Capturing this opportunity requires that the concepts of research and information change. Marketing executives are disenfranchised from available advertising and media research. A growing majority express dissatisfaction with their ability to define the effectiveness of advertising and media through available resources.

Findings from research conducted by *Myers Reports* confirm that fully 95% of all marketing executives from major national advertisers are dissatisfied with available research on advertising's impact on sales. A substantial majority support a shift away from traditional quantitative measures to research that better evaluates the impact of advertising on actual purchase decisions.

Many researchers in the ad business have become convinced that the vast proportion of research we have available to us has proven incapable of providing answers to the most fundamental questions of advertising effectiveness. Research too often answers the mundane questions of audience size with a degree of accuracy questioned by many, and it seems to lack any real value for answering the deep sociological issues that drive to the very heart of advertising's role and purpose.

We have a wealth of information, but very little knowledge. The information we have is produced to satisfy the needs of specialists -- highly trained and skilled practitioners of a singular component of the advertising process. The advertising industry's research resources have been created to serve advertising's products -- creative and media -- rather than its service -- generating sales results.

We have Nielsen and Arbitron ratings for television and radio media buying, SMRB, MRI and PIB for magazine buying, Starch for measuring ad recall, LNA (Leading National Advertisers Reports) for tracking competitive ad spending, PRIZM for identifying audience clusters. But we have little research that brings the process of advertising together under one umbrella to enhance wisdom, organize consumer and trade marketing, coordinate creative concept and execution and define how media selection converts to consumer response.

We have in the ad business today an *information tapeworm* that feeds on itself. The more we stuff into it, the weaker and less satisfied we become. Neil Postman points out: "Technology increases the available supply of information. As the supply is increased, control mechanisms are strained. Additional control mechanisms are needed to cope with new information. When additional control mechanisms are themselves technical, they, in turn, further increase the supply of information. When the supply of information is no longer controllable, a general breakdown in psychic tranquility and social purpose occurs."

With the extraordinary research resources advertisers have available to them on advertising creative and media, they have become more and more dissatisfied with the product of advertising.

In Postman's *Technopoly*, he suggests: "Like the sorcerer's apprentice, we are awash in information. Information has become a form of garbage, not only incapable of answering the most fundamental human questions but barely useful in providing coherent direction to the solution of even mundane questions. The tie between information and... purpose has been severed." Marketers and media are faced with information overload and information chaos. As Postman points out, "There are very few problems that arise as a result of insufficient information. Yet, incomprehensible problems mount and [executives] stand firm in believing that what the world needs is yet more information. They are driven to fill our lives with the quest to access more information. We have never before been faced with an information glut and we have hardly had time to reflect on its consequences."

The consequences for the marketing, advertising and media industries have been apparent. The perception of advertising's value has declined; media's share of the marketing pie has dramatically shrunk; the advertising industry is in crisis. The marketing and advertising industry *must* respond to the criticism implied by the high level of marketers' dissatisfaction with things as they are. Researchers must focus on how advertising works and how marketers can use media to produce results.

The very words "research" and "researchers" have taken on baggage that is detrimental to the marketing and advertising industries. Many marketers have lost sight of the true role of research, which is, simply, to be a *tool* for decision-makers. Research is intended to be a servant, not a master. It serves at the direction of the decision-maker; the decision-maker should not act at the direction of research.

The role of research is to be a tool for increasing wisdom and knowledge. Yet, many view *the acquisition of data* as the end rather than the means for increasing knowledge. Just as the computer and technology require human input and direction, research requires human interpretation and analysis. Research unto itself is not knowledge; it enhances knowledge when interpreted by an executive who is thoroughly versed in the marketplace, the objectives and the issues being evaluated. Marketers today are too frequently losing access to valuable knowledge because those developing, implementing and determining the value of the research are focusing on the data without an adequate understanding of the issues or objectives being measured.

The result is that we have an abundance of research *data* but a dramatic decline in knowledge. Research is losing its value as a decision-making tool.

Perceptions toward the value of research are also declining as a direct result of overly dogmatic reliance on highly restrictive methodological requirements that no longer are always pertinent or valid, but upon which many researchers steadfastly insist.

Researchers would argue that the validity of any research study is determined by its adherence to tried and true methodological rules. I disagree. Valid methodology is essential, but too often, valid and valuable knowledge is lost because obtaining that knowledge required going outside the bounds of traditional research practices. The changes in society, in media, and in marketing require that we establish new standards, sometimes on a project-by-project basis. Research must be brought back under the rule and direction of those who require the knowledge... not those who are evaluating the data.

For example, researchers typically hold that a 50% response rate is necessary for a study to be considered reliable. I recently reviewed a study where the total universe studied was 4,000.

Questionnaires were mailed to all 4,000. Members of the group were relatively similar in their characteristics. Considering that studies of several hundred people are offered as statistically representative of millions, the 900 returned questionnaires should be considered a reliable base of information. The issue for researchers, though, is not the value of the information but whether those responding differ significantly from those who do not respond. Several corporate research directors rejected the study because the response rate was not the 50% they demanded. Nearly 25% *of the total universe* were included in the survey, but the study was rejected due to a lack of adherence to inappropriately restrictive rules of research. These same research executives will accept the results of a focus group involving only 10 - 12 people if it adheres to their restrictive methodological rules. If the same study had been mailed to 200 individuals and 100 had responded, it would have been more acceptable than a study with 900 respondents! When corporate management empowers researchers to determine the *value of information* it is misplaced and destructive empowerment.

When I began consulting with companies in the early 1980s, I recommended a broad quantitative survey of a client's customers to ascertain the major issues the client faced. Based upon the results of this survey, I conducted extensive personal and telephone interviews with the client's customers to gain a more in-depth understanding of the dynamics underlying their responses to the survey. Once these dynamics were understood and issues identified, I conducted focus groups of customers to review strategic issues and discuss the pros and cons of alternative strategies for my client. The process was logical and worked extremely well.

Yet, I've consistently been told that traditional and accepted research techniques <u>dictate</u> that focus groups should be the first step in the process, followed by personal interviews and concluded with a quantitative survey. Different intentions. Different methodologies. Yet, some traditionalists remain locked into existing paradigms, rejecting alternative approaches and the improved knowledge they may generate.

It <u>is</u> necessary for the marketing community to have an immune system to protect itself from invalid information. Without a well-functioning immune system, an organism cannot manage cellular growth. But marketers have allowed those responsible for *gathering* information to determine whether that information is valid or invalid -- wanted or unwanted. This is misplaced responsibility, and causes a total breakdown of the system.

The emphasis on controls and methodological purity rather than knowledge and enhanced decision-making is a destructive force in advertising today.

SEARCHING FOR ADVERTISING'S HOLY GRAIL

While advertising agency and media executives often have discussed approaches for measuring advertising effectiveness, they ultimately have concluded that such a quest for the "holy grail of knowledge" is an impossible task. What's more, it appears to many in the industry that such a study is unnecessary.

With media revenues growing in the double digits each year, why conjure up a research study that could conceivably call the value of advertising into question? Inotherwords, "if it ain't broken, why fix it?" The role of media research has been to provide a comparative tool for determining the value of one magazine vs. another based upon circulation, or one television program vs. another based upon ratings. Advertisers have accepted (several even demanded) ad recall and likability tests that measure the creative product. But while the ad business may not have been "broken," it has been slowly eroded by a lack of clear insight into marketers' true needs and spending shifts. American auto manufacturers faced the same crossroads in the 1970s and 80s and are just now responding in the 1990s.

The agency business succeeds only to the degree that it successfully promotes its clients' businesses. Its prime interest should be increasing sales for others, bettering clients' competitive standing and enlarging clients' profits. For the agency to be highly valued it must see through its clients' eyes and become an essential and trusted part of its clients' management teams.

As major agencies went public and were bought through leveraged buyouts in the 1970s and 1980s, financial self-interest became the primary management focus. Ostensibly, agencies remained committed to the clients' needs and interests, but realistically their place as "essential and trusted" advisors was eroded as their clients increasingly questioned the contribution of the ad agency to their total marketing efforts.

Just as several major corporations began hiring in-house medical staffs and outside HMOs to provide employees with the majority of their medical needs, corporations also have formed in-house ad agencies and hired specialized media buying services, creative boutiques and production houses to perform advertising tasks. In the United States, Boclaro, the in-house arm of Bristol-Myers Squibb, and other corporate in-house advertising units have expressed a willingness to take on work for outside, non-competitive companies.

In Europe, the giant pharmaceutical company Ciba-Geigy set up Allcom Business Communications to offer advertising and media buying services to other advertisers. Allcom also provides graphic and corporate design, trade fairs and exhibitions, collateral material and promotional services. With a staff of 140 and revenues of $14 million, Allcom is the third largest Swiss agency. German manufacturer Daimler-Benz, which makes everything from Mercedes-Benz automobiles to airplane engines, has created Debis Marketing Services to handle internal divisions as well as external clients. Their idea is to be different from traditional ad agencies *by being present during every stage of the marketing process.*

Advertising today is heading in a directly opposite direction from the Debis Marketing Services model. It is no longer perceived as a single integrated *process.* Instead it is several separate and distinct *tasks:* television writing, magazine writing, radio writing, graphics design, illustration, photography, television production, radio production, print production, television media, radio media, outdoor, magazine media, newspaper media, account management, traffic, media research, marketing research, etc.

Agencies today are operating on the basis that the changes in their business are driven by declining margins and shrinking profitability. Financial management, responsible to shareholders and over-leveraged owners, looks at an agency's staff service departments as cost centers with profit-making potential. Today, few major advertising agencies believe that their individual departments cannot be operated as separate profit centers.

Virtually every major and mid-sized agency has clients for which they provide ala carte creative and/or media services. DDB/Needham, Saatchi & Saatchi and N.W. Ayer have announced an aggressive push to attract media-only business.

It is highly likely that several major agencies will "unbundle" their media departments during the next several years, positioning agencies to compete with independent media buying services and to offer a viable alternative to clients who are considering in-house capabilities.

Unbundling also enables major agency groups such as Saatchi & Saatchi, Omnicom (which owns BBDO, DDB/Needham and Goodby, Berlin, Silverstein) and WPP (consisting of J. Walter Thompson, Ogilvy & Mather and Scali, McCabe & Sloves) to combine the back room administrative costs of their different agencies.

By the end of the decade, a few major media buying organizations will emerge, representing a large percentage of total national buying.

The very concept of "consolidation" of media services is a misnomer. While it represents the combining of the media capabilities of multiple agencies in response to financial and tactical business needs, in reality it causes the further *separation* of media from other functions within the agency.

Television commercial production is another highly specialized area in which agencies are pressured by clients to reduce costs. Jordan Kalfus, executive producer of independent production firm Harmony Pictures, commented at a convention of production experts that marketers are increasingly considering their agencies little more than suppliers, and agencies in turn treat production firms in the same fashion. Complicating the industry's difficulties has been a trend toward clients becoming competitors, says Mr. Kalfus, "as the agencies aggressively push for their own in-house production." Advertisers, too, are exploring in-house production options and are opening direct relations with the production firms, bypassing their agencies in the actual production of commercials.

The inevitability of further separation of agency services demonstrates the conflict between the realities of the past 30 years and the dynamics of the next 30. A senior media director from a leading agency succinctly stated the problem: "Consolidation will change the entire face of media buying and planning for clients, agencies and media. Agencies will be more vulnerable and there will be casualties along the line. Media sales forces will be smaller. There will be fewer communications among media and agencies. The clients will suffer, but they have let the lion out of the cage by cutting compensation."

NOW IS THE TIME TO ACT

Scientists recently discovered a process in the body's immune system called "anergy." It has commonly been believed that, when an invading virus attacks the body, white blood cells race to the point of invasion, surrounding and destroying the invading virus. It is now known that the white blood cells do charge to the point of incursion but they do not immediately attack. Instead, they wait passively "on the sidelines" in the "anergic state," depending upon a second signal from the brain to confirm the virus and authorize the white cells to attack.

In the advertising business, we are settled in the anergic state. We know there are problems. Trade and consumer promotional spending has invaded the marketing budget. There is a virus attacking the health of the advertising system. But efforts to respond have been passive at best. The industry is waiting for a signal to take action. But what action? And who is responsible for sending the signal? Becoming overly dependent upon research for addressing issues of advertising effectiveness is analogous to assigning the white blood cells the job of the brain. We stand in danger, in the advertising business, of becoming so reliant on information and its methodological purity that we lose our ability to think intelligently and logically about that information.

Too many executives wait passively on the sidelines accepting business as usual as a virus eats away at the health of their business. For the advertising industry to renew its vitality and dominant role in the marketing process, it must refocus all its energies on improving measures of effectiveness and centralizing all the resources available to an advertiser under a single management umbrella charged with the responsibility for bringing logical cohesion and direction to the marketer's information resources.

Another extraordinary discovery in the medical community is that a gene called p53 is a cell's primary defensive weapon against the malignant growth of cancerous cells that can grow without check and move from one organ to another until the health of the organism is destroyed. The p53 gene can sense the first signs of damage to chromosomes and prevent a cell from doing anything further until DNA enzymes can act and repair the damage.

The advertising industry requires its own version of the p53 gene -- a police agent who has a view of a marketers' total strategy and who can recognize and act to stop any destructive elements that are negatively effecting the success of that strategy and the health of the marketer.

KNOWLEDGE RESOURCES

In the 1970s and 1980s, the differences between "personnel" managers and "human resources" managers became apparent. Personnel is a simple synonym for workers. It does not describe the complex task of responding to the very real issues faced by modern corporations. The human resources manager is a far more apt description of the role and responsibilities of these senior executives.

In this same context, research should be recognized as a synonym for information -- a tool. Companies today require Knowledge Resources managers, reflecting the contemporary role of those individuals charged with responsibility for developing research, interpreting research, defining its uses, and integrating research into the advertising and marketing process. These individuals may employ research managers, but the distinction must be made between research -- which provides information -- and knowledge, which is the master -- served by research.

What our industry needs are more Knowledge Resources managers. Like the general medical practitioner, an advertising agency Knowledge Resources Manager knows the client intimately, can be thoroughly involved in every step of the marketing, creative and media process, and can assess all the various information streams and their relevance to the clients' objectives. The Knowledge Resources Manager will provide a valuable service for marketers.

Knowledge Resources executives will elevate the role and perception of research by better defining its purposes and goals. The goal of meaningful marketing and advertising research is not more data. It is not information. Rather, the goal is to increase knowledge about marketers' goals and objectives, and the effectiveness of marketing communications programs in achieving these goals.

The dependence of advertising executives on standardized data resources at the expense of analytical and logical processes is the product of the many changes that occurred in the 1970s and '80s. Through Knowledge Resources managers, research will return to its rightful place as a *tool* for guiding logical thought and decision-making. Knowledge Resources managers can take responsibility for bringing the appropriate arms of the client and the agency together to facilitate improved communications. Knowledge Resources managers are, in effect, agency point persons, responsible for interfacing the client's objectives with the agency's recommendations.

More than an account executive, the Knowledge Resources Manager must be equally adept at interpreting research and writing a client's marketing strategies. Knowledge Resources managers must be responsible for triggering coordinated efforts to address the problems faced by marketers in their consideration of advertising as a marketing tool.

ADVERTISING'S GENERAL PRACTITIONER

A relatively new development in the advertising business has been the introduction of Account Planning, which *Adweek Magazine* referred to as "a kind of calculated risk-taking that combines quantitative research with gut instinct ....Account planning takes cold, hard research data and adds a human dimension." The *Adweek* article adds: "Because they represent the consumer -- the missing link between the creative department and the client -- planners have become a new, increasingly powerful breed within agencies."

The account planning system is a progenitor of Knowledge Resources Planners. Account planning was imported from England, where agencies have hired university professors, philosophy writers and mathematics theorists to provide them with new insights into their clients' marketplaces. In the United States, Chiat/Day/Mojo was the first agency to introduce the concept and, in the last several years, the approach has expanded mostly to young agencies that have primarily been dependent upon their creative reputation.

Account planning is knowledge management. It is a necessary step in the evolution of advertising agencies. Account planning is viewed, however, as a means of integrating "cold, hard research data" with the creative process. Several major agencies, including Foote, Cone & Belding, Ketchum, DDB/Needham and Ogilvy & Mather are exploring and slowly introducing the concept.

This is precisely the concept against which Jerry Della Femina protested. Many agency executives still question whether account planners deserve to be given a central role in the creative planning process. Says *Adweek,* "However much they share the creative's love of advertising, a planner's job is to bring order to one of the few places in American business where leaps of faith are still accepted, if not revered. As a result, planners bring a certain humility to the task. It didn't take an account planner to write "Blondes have more fun" or to create the Marlboro man either. And some agency executives question whether account planners have earned an integral role in agency operations, or if they simply are a fashionable tool for the '90s."

The creative product is so central to the ad agency business that agencies are interpreting their clients' concerns with advertising effectiveness as a question of how the creative process is conducted. In response, agencies are considering adapting more quantitative approaches to the creative process. Naturally, this strikes a wooden stake into the very heart of many creative directors. The account planner's appropriate role is to be the agency's equivalent of the general practitioner, becoming extraordinarily knowledgeable about the "patient," and becoming equally comfortable in *all* facets of the advertising agency's services. To be most effective, the very concept of the account planner should be reversed, and the title changed to "Knowledge Resources Manager." Rather than integrating research into the creative process, the Knowledge Resources Manager should be responsible for integrating "gut instinct" and creativity into the media and research arms of the agency.

The role of Knowledge Resources Manager should be to bring a thorough understanding of the client's objectives to all facets of the advertising process. The word *process* must be emphasized. Agencies must view their work as a composite, merging together research, the creative product, media and production to achieve strategic solutions. To best serve marketers, this should be approached as an interlinked process, not the sum of many independent parts.

Creative and media departments should work together with a well-researched plan focused on implementing strategies and achieving clearly stated objectives. The Knowledge Resources Manager -- and client executives themselves -- should represent the voice of the client, serving as the p53 molecule protecting the organism against cancerous agents.

The difference between Account Planning and Knowledge Management is that the latter represents a total integration of agency services under a single integrative and protective umbrella, not simply the introduction of basic marketing research principles into the creative process. In fact, research has always been an integral part of the creative process.

Agencies traditionally have considered research to be a key part of their ability to develop meaningful campaigns. The knowledge/account planning system is, in its best form, an opportunity to enhance the *quality* of advertising agency management through improved exploration of the market and more focused client-agency relationships. The knowledge management system is consistent with the Deming theories of management.

W. Edwards Deming, who is considered the father of quality management, is a professor of statistics, yet the procedures and management techniques attributed to him identify statistics as a tool for supporting "process" rather than a measure of success or failure. Deming's Theory for Management is an appropriate doctrine for advertising agency executives.

THE 14 POINT THEORY FOR MANAGEMENT
W. Edwards Deming
Reprinted from the Kappa Sigma *Caduceus*

1. Create constancy of purpose toward improvement of product and service, with the aim to become competitive and to stay in business, and to provide jobs.
2. Adopt a new philosophy. We are in a new economic age. Western management must awaken to the challenge, must learn their responsibilities, and take on leadership for change.
3. Cease dependence on inspection to achieve quality. Eliminate the need for inspection on a mass basis by building quality into the product in the first place.
4. End the practice of awarding business solely on the basis of price. Instead, minimize total cost. Move toward a single supplier for any one item, on a long-term relationship of loyalty and trust.
5. Improve constantly and forever the system of production and service, to improve quality and productivity, and thus constantly decrease costs.
6. Institute training on the job to make better use of all employees.
7. Institute leadership (see point 12). The aim of leadership should be to help people and machines and gadgets do a better job. Leadership of management is in need of an overhaul, as well as leadership of production workers.
8. Drive out fear, so that everyone may work effectively for the company.
9. Break down barriers between departments. People in research,

design, sales and production must work as a team to foresee problems of production, and in use, that may be encountered with the product or service.

10. Eliminate slogans, exhortations and targets for the work force that ask for zero defects or ask for new levels off productivity without providing methods.

11. a. Eliminate work standards (quotas) on the factory floor. Substitute leadership.
b. Eliminate management by objective. Eliminate management by numbers, numerical goals. Substitute leadership.

12. a. Remove barriers that rob the hourly worker of his right to pride of workmanship. The responsibility of supervisors must be changed from sheer numbers to quality.
b. Remove barriers that rob people in management and in engineering of their right to pride of workmanship. This means, inter alia, abolishment of the annual merit rating and of management by objective, management by the numbers.

13. Institute a vigorous program of education and self-improvement.

14. Clearly define top management's permanent commitment to quality and productivity and its obligation to implement these principles. Put everybody in the company to work to accomplish the transformation. The transformation is everybody's job.

Some minor revisions are required to apply the points to ad agencies. In point three, insert "recall" and "likeability" in place of "inspection." In point four, apply the concept to media resources and relationships. In point seven, think of "production workers" as all employees. In point nine, add media department and account teams. In point 11, replace "factory floor" with "media department." Demand *leadership* in every aspect of management rather than measured quantitative achievements. These same points can be appropriately applied to marketers and media companies alike; they are intended for every business.

Instituting Deming's recommendations are a key to success in the 1990s. They are particularly relevant to advertising agencies *and* to media companies. However, agencies, caught in the over-leveraged crunch of the 1990s, have dramatically cut back on support staffs. Corporations have driven down agency compensation, reducing the agencies' ability to provide extensive and expensive marketing support. The knowledge planning concept, put in perspective, represents putting Deming's philosophy into place throughout the agency with a lead expert serving as the agency's communications link for each individual client. It requires a reprioritizing and repackaging of an agency's services, emphasizing the *process* of gaining and using *knowledge* as a tool for leadership rather than statistics as a substitute for performance.

COMPETING ON CAPABILITIES

The *Harvard Business Review* of April, 1992 provides a manifest for marketing, advertising and media management. The article, *Competing on Capabilities: The New Rules of Corporate Strategy*, calls for "a new conception of corporate strategy that we call capabilities-based competition." This concept "emphasizes behavior -- the organizational practices and business processes in which capabilities are rooted -- as the primary object of strategy and therefore focuses its managerial attention on the infrastructure that supports capabilities. This subtle distinction has made all the difference between exceptional and average performance."

The four principles of capabilities-based competition are:

1. The building blocks of corporate strategy are not products and markets but business processes.

2. Competitive success depends on transforming a company's key processes into strategic capabilities that consistently provide superior value to the consumer. [The consumer here can be the advertiser, or it can be the advertiser's ultimate customers.]

3. Companies create these capabilities by making strategic investments in a support infrastructure that links and transcends traditional SBUs (standard business units) and existing corporate functions.

4. Because capabilities necessarily cross functions, the champion of a capabilities-based strategy is the CEO.

Further quoting the article, "A capability is a set of business processes strategically understood. Every company has business processes that deliver value to the customer. But few think of them as the primary object of strategy. Capabilities-based competitors identify their key business processes, manage them centrally, and invest in them heavily, looking for a long-term payback.

"What transforms a set of individual business processes...into a strategic capability? The key is to connect them to real customer needs. A capability is strategic only when it begins and ends with the customer.

"Of course, just about every company these days claims to be 'close to the customer.' But there is a qualitative difference in the customer focus of capabilities-driven competitors. These companies conceive of the organization as a giant feedback loop that begins and ends with identifying the needs of the customer and ends with satisfying them.

"Weaving business processes together into organizational capabilities in this way also mandates a new logic of vertical integration. At a time when cost pressures are pushing many companies to outsource more and more activities, capabilities-based competitors are integrating vertically to ensure that they, not a supplier or distributor, control the performance of key business processes.

"Even when a company doesn't actually own every link of the capability chain, the capabilities-based competitor works to tie these parts into its own business systems."

The opportunity inherent in the agency and media businesses is to create capabilities-based organizations. In an agency, the knowledge resources system empowers a point person to pull together all the capabilities available from the client, agency, research companies, media companies, and the client's promotional and marketing resources. The point person can focus his or her energies on integrating all aspects of the process of communicating the client's message to the consumer. In this way, the agency serves as the link, bringing together marketing, research, media and creative with the single objective of developing creative solutions to a client's marketing needs. Rather than emphasizing the agency's products (i.e. a commercial, creative strategy or media plan) the agency is competing based upon its capabilities and processes of focusing on its clients' needs and organizing all its services to meet those objectives. This totally changes the measures by which the value of a media plan is measured; it alters the measure of the agency's creative product away from awards, recall and likeability measures and toward its effectiveness in fulfilling specific client marketing objectives.

James C. Reilly, general manager, Marketing Services & Communications for IBM wrote on the concept of integrated marketing communications in *Advertiser* magazine, the publication of the *Association of National Advertisers:*

"Where companies are always on the alert for the latest 'magic bullet' that promises competitive advantage, Integrated Marketing Communications appears to be holding its own, albeit tenuously, on the slippery slope of acceptability.

"Some call it 'one-voice marketing'; others call it 'seamless communications.' Integrated Marketing Communications is generally viewed as the deliberate and thoughtful orchestration of different communications activities to effectively deliver targeted messages to defined audiences. Definitions aside, integration has become especially critical in an age where mass media has arguably lost its primacy, where the growth of niche marketing is gaining momentum, and where marketing budgets are under intense pressure....

"Consumers are confounded by thousands of messages a day. We didn't want to be lost in that media clutter -- clutter that doesn't just come from advertising, but from direct mail, sales promotion, and publicity campaigns as well. By integrating our communications, we hoped to clarify our messages and better coordinate our efforts."

Reilly went on to point out that IBM thinks of itself "as a complete in-house 'agency,' whose talents are leveraged by several hundred large and small outside suppliers....Our Communications Planning department, acting like an account executive from our internal 'agency,' helps the sponsor integrate all elements of marketing communications into a single solid support plan."

The question that advertising agencies must answer is whether they can compete as one of "several hundred vendors" or if they can effectively demonstrate their ability to provide the most effective "integration of all elements of marketing communications into a single support plan." This does not require that the agency maintain all these services in-house. In fact, it is likely that most agencies will not retain fully integrated in-house operations. But they must take responsibility for coordination and integration if they are to maintain their traditional role and responsibility for "producing ideas for increasing clients' sales, reputations and profits."

The future trend is toward emphasis on the Knowledge Resources Manager's role as a coordinator and integrator of the marketing communications process. The Knowledge Resources Manager can be employed by an agency, the advertiser itself, an independent consulting group, or even by a media company.

Those advertising agencies that emphasize one or two, or even three specialized services but also coordinate *all* marketing processes under a single umbrella through Knowledge Resources Planning will be the legitimate heirs to the Ogilvy, Burnett and Cone mandate that advertising's role should be to sell the clients' products and services. The role of those agencies emphasizing ala carte services without integrated capabilities management will be to *sell* their own specific products or services and to compete on a *commodity basis* with other vendors of these products and services.

A key issue for marketing decision-makers is whether or not they are willing to involve media companies and ad agencies in their confidential strategic planning process. Many corporations have organized to reduce the amount of direct contact among brand managers, ad agency and media personnel. Instead, corporate advertising departments are responsible for this function, separating the agency from direct knowledge of a product's total marketing activities and the behind-the-scenes budgeting process.

INTEGRATION OF CAPABILITIES

Corporations also depend upon agency media departments, in-house media groups or independent media buying services to provide them with recommendations on the most cost-efficient media buys to reach specific target audiences. But how often do senior television or magazine *company* executives meet with a *team* of agency media, creative and research executives to discuss an advertiser's specific strategic needs and to develop creative ideas to fulfill those needs? *Virtually never.*

A marketing research director of one top 10 advertising agency has responsibility for identifying strategic issues relevant to specific products. Since 1985, this individual's department has been reduced from 12 people to one person. His responsibilities, which were once devoted 85% to existing clients and 15% to new business development, have been virtually reversed. And *never* in the past ten years has this marketing expert been called in by his agency's media department to meet directly with media company executives in order to discuss how the media can most creatively contribute to a client's marketing needs.

If the Knowledge Resources Manager truly understands the marketer's business and can effectively interpret the objectives...if teams of individuals from creative, media, research, production, etc., all equally knowledgeable about the client's objectives and equally focused on fulfilling these objectives, can work together... if external media, research and promotional resources that ultimately are funded by the marketer's programs, can be pulled together and their expertise tapped... the product of the agency will be radically altered and advertisers' perceived value of their agencies will be dramatically enhanced.

Service organizations such as Marketing Resources Plus, which package administrative services for agencies, advertisers and media companies, are also contributing to the expansion of partnerships among media, agencies and their clients. MRP's computerized programs assure that all parties are operating with the same information resources, and that they are equally committed to delivering full value for the dollars invested. According to consultants, upwards of 10% - 50% of media invoices (varying by medium) delivered to agencies by media companies require some form of adjustment or correction. Current systems and structures tend to impose undue costs upon the agencies to correct these sytematic discrepancies, although funding should be the responsibility of the media and the advertiser. New systems now in development will assure full value is delivered by media.

ARE MEDIA COMPANIES PREPARED FOR CHANGE?

The challenges faced by advertising agencies parallel the issues that media companies must also address in the future. Media have traditionally *not* been viewed as *marketing partners* by advertisers or their agencies. Rather, they have been perceived as commodities designed to deliver a message as inexpensively as possible to a particular audience. Media sales representatives are not typically challenged to develop new and creative means of addressing a client's specific marketing needs.

No research system is in place that regularly tracks the success of a medium in achieving the client's original marketing goals. Media companies, which may receive millions of dollars in advertising from an individual advertiser, are only rarely aware of that advertiser's objectives, goals, measurement criteria or other marketing activities of which media advertising is just one component.

Most media companies' sales organizations are unaware of an advertiser's intentions to purchase their specific medium until the agency's media planner or buyer advises the media sales representative that "budgets are available." Media salespeople are highly paid to respond to this "availability" request, providing agency buyers with basic information on audiences and costs.

The buyer's job is then to review the various options and to negotiate purchase decisions. Media buyers at the largest advertising agencies are typically responsible for negotiating a single medium and, as in the case of network television dayparts, a component of a single medium. Magazine buying also has a parallel to the network daypart arrangement. Several large agencies have buyers who work only on "women's specialty magazines," or "newsweeklies." The media buying process is highly specialized and fragmented.

The primary revenue focus for media companies historically has been based on "share of spending." Radio or television network and station management want to know what share of each client's spending they received in each negotiation. Their first involvement on a piece of business is typically when the buyer contacts the salesperson to announce an interest in buying. It may then take several hours to several weeks before a deal is closed, but negotiations are intense and based on available inventory and the cost of that inventory. Each negotiation is different and dependent upon the client's and agency's negotiating skills, relationships between media sellers and buyers, total spending, willingness to be flexible about inventory, placement and several other factors.

In times when television inventory was tight -- not available -- stations and networks could immediately *jack up* the rates; when the marketplace was "soft," rates would be lowered. In television, rates could change from day to day and deal to deal.

This approach to selling has worked well for media. By focusing aggressively on building strong relationships with the media buyer and planner, sales representatives are assured of being made aware of every available "piece of business" and are given a fair opportunity to negotiate for a share of that business.

Media sales representatives' efforts to meet directly with advertisers historically have been discouraged by advertising agency media executives. Clients themselves were, in the past, often reluctant to meet with media company salespeople, having turned over decision-making responsibility to the agency or media buying service. Magazine sales executives effectively circumvented this restriction by developing marketing programs and support services that required client input. Television and radio sales executives, on the other hand, often reinforced the "hands off" policy when calling on advertisers by often launching into "us vs. them" cost efficiency pitches that were clearly in the domain of the agency.

The traditional segregation of media representatives from their advertisers' marketing objectives reflects patterns established in the earliest days of the newspaper space peddler. Since most cities boasted two, three and even four major newspapers, each concentrated on defending itself at the expense of its competitors.

As each new medium -- magazines, radio and television -- emerged, similar patterns developed. Selling became highly competitive -- each medium against all other media and each station or publication against all others. Every man for himself. As national media became available through expanded magazine circulation and broadcast networks, these patterns became institutionalized.

Media associations such as the Newspaper Advertising Bureau, the Magazine Publishers of America, and Television Bureau of Advertising devoted their resources to generating propaganda and research that was focused on their medium's individual strengths and their competitors' weaknesses. Little thought was given to the cumulative negative impact over many years of this strategy on overall perceptions of advertising and media. In all fairness to media companies and trade associations, the reality that demand for media time and space exceeded supply in the past 100 years justified today's buying and selling organizational structure at agencies and media companies. Media management was not required to be overly concerned about building the base of revenues for advertising as an industry or even for their own medium. Agency media departments literally had to fight with media to assure that their clients received a competitively fair deal and to hold down year-to-year price increases.

Still today, television and radio media are bought and sold mostly as commodities, with media sellers and agency media buyers negotiating costs based upon highly restrictive criteria established by agency media planners. Media planners receive a set of objectives from a senior media executive and agency account managers. What may begin as in-depth customer profiles and marketing objectives are ultimately reduced to straight demographic data, such as "women 25-54" or "men 18-49." Once it is decided which media will be used (which is typically completed without consultation with the media themselves) specific media purchases are made based primarily upon comparative costs of reaching the pre-determined audiences. Media sales representatives aggressively negotiate with agency buyers who pit salesperson against salesperson to drive the costs down as low as possible. Supply and demand shifts control of this process back and forth from buyer to seller. From the mid-1950s to the late-1980s demand has exceeded supply, giving the upper hand to the media and making the effective television/radio negotiator a prized and valuable person at ad agencies.

By the late 1980s, it was becoming increasingly clear that the balance of supply/demand power had shifted from the seller to the buyer, motivating the largest, most savvy advertisers to exert stronger control over the media buying process to extract the greatest discounts and competitive advantages.

As marketers extended their brand names to multiple product lines and introduced new products targeted to ever more narrow audiences in the 1980s, changes in media served marketers' expanded needs. The most dramatic and visible of these changes was cable television. Today, cable wires pass 85% of all U.S. homes with nearly 65% of all homes connected by this cable wire to an extensive menu of television choices. By 1999, *Myers Reports* projects that cable will reach into 85% of all homes, most connected by fiber optic wire, which will radically expand the variety of programming options.

In 1970, 2,500 individual cable television systems served 4.5 million cable subscribers. By 1990, 10,500 systems served nearly 60 million subscribers. During the same period, the number of traditional broadcast television stations grew from 682 to more than 1,000. In 1970 there were three broadcast networks: ABC, NBC and CBS. Defying forecasters who predicted the demise of one or more networks by 1990, a fourth network, FOX-TV, is thriving today and other part-time, or unwired, networks continue to serve advertisers' needs.

CNN, MTV AND THE NEW WIRED WORLD

From the very beginning, cable television networks were successful in gaining acceptance among national advertisers. Their success resulted in no small measure because advertisers and agency media buyers were eager for a low cost alternative to broadcast networks. Although cable networks delivered audiences that were often only 2% - 5% of the size of broadcast network audiences, advertisers were willing to support these networks because comparative costs-per-thousand viewers were, on average, half those of broadcast networks. Although cable spending was barely a flea on the broadcast network dog in the early 1980s, by the 1990s it had grown to become a competitor to be reckoned with.

An important part of cable's success was its ability to benefit from its position as a low cost alternative to broadcast networks while offering advertisers more targeting capabilities to reach specific audience groups. Cable networks such as MTV, Arts & Entertainment and ESPN sought out advertisers who had particular interests in reaching their unique audiences, packaging their networks as special opportunities to reach these audiences with high frequency in a highly focused programming environment. This combination was extremely productive. Many cable networks were able to define their own audience strengths and marketplace niche, justifying low ratings by focusing on advertisers who targeted their advertising to those audiences.

Superstation TBS, USA Network and Turner's TNT Network provided larger ratings and broader audiences, giving cable the imprimatur of network-like programming. Several networks continued to rely on broadcast network reruns, but viewers consistently demonstrated their willingness to return time and again to these programs, and advertisers were assured that their ads would air in a familiar surrounding.

Throughout the 1980s, revenues for TBS, MTV, ESPN, Arts & Entertainment and Cable News Network, among others, grew rapidly. A few forward thinking ad agency media executives became early and aggressive cable supporters, some building their careers on their vision of rapid audience shifts. Most advertising agencies jumped on the cable bandwagon. Those ad agency media executives who were cable kickers, and there were many, often found that they got the boot instead. Younger executives with a better understanding of the growing importance of cable to the television viewer moved into positions of authority.

Cable grew. Programming improved. Ratings increased. Cable networks began aggressive marketing campaigns to attract viewers to made-for-cable movies and specials. Audiences grew even larger and advertisers followed.

As cable grew more successful, the cable network advertising time buying and selling process turned toward the traditional patterns of the network television business. Ad agency media departments gained increasing control over the buying decision, packaging cable conceptually with broadcast networks. By emphasizing quantitative size of the audience and the cost of cable spots, the perceived value of cable's audience targeting strengths were eroded. Cable networks emphasized their audience ratings growth as a primary selling tool. Agency media buyers focused on cable's cost-per-thousand viewers, grouping networks according to broad audience age and sex demographics.

This became problematic for a network such as MTV. An "adults

18-49" target audience might typically be used as a buying specification by an ad agency network media buyer. While MTV effectively delivers the 18-24 component of that audience, it prices itself at a premium for that audience. Several other networks deliver substantially larger numbers of adults 25-49, but underdeliver the 18-24 audience.

An agency media buyer might buy only those networks that are efficient based on their total 18-49 numbers. If the goal is to deliver 100 gross rating points (each rating point equals one percent of the target audience), an advertiser might receive 100 adult 18-49 rating points while hypothetically receiving 110 GRPs among adults 25-49 while only receiving 85 GRPs among adults 18-24. Ideally, agency media buyers adjust accordingly, but executives from several highly targeted networks suggest that the buying process should be more defined so as not to penalize networks that reach concentrations of highly targeted audiences.

What's more, these highly specialized networks appear locked into doing business in ways that do not serve their best long-term interests. They remain, in essence, commodities whose pricing is largely dependent on broadcast network pricing and media buyers' needs for low cost alternatives. While they may provide specific advertisers highly targeted and specialized marketing benefits, they are very limited in their ability to develop or support these benefits. Cable networks have limited funds to support their sales and marketing organizations. The realities of business dictate that the majority of these resources be used to support salespeople who call on advertising agencies' media buyers so that they can extract the largest possible share of the available cable network television pot.

It would place an enormous financial burden on networks to hire and train experienced marketing executives and support ala carte promotional programs for individual advertisers. Compounding this problem is the reality that when networks do make this effort, the actual media buy is typically placed in the hands of the advertising agency media department, which is charged with the responsibility of assuring that the advertiser pay no more than the going market rates. Advertisers have not been sufficiently motivated to pay for enhanced marketing services that media companies may offer. Media companies have not succeeded in clearly demonstrating value for special services beyond market negotiated prices.

Entrepreneurial companies will take advantage of the increasing costs of conducting business. Agents will develop multi-media sales organizations which consolidate administrative services, research and marketing support for emerging media companies. This will be especially advantageous in the cable television industry, where growing networks can be merged into a single ratings and administrative package.

MAGAZINES -- TRADITIONAL VALUES VS. SPACE BROKERS

Unlike television, magazines traditionally established rate cards to which they steadfastly held, enabling them to focus on unique editorial and marketing strengths. They positioned their unique relationships with readers, and often sold the *concept* of magazines and the category in which they competed (such as "women's service," "specialty sports" or "newsweeklies") as valuable marketing vehicles.

In the late 1980s and early 1990s, as the economy worsened, the numbers of magazines competing in each category increased, advertising budgets declined and several magazines began aggressive discounting. The first magazine to "break rate card," was *McCall's,* now owned by New York Times Magazines but then owned by Lang Communications. Dale Lang, chairman of Lang, was roundly criticized by other publishers, but the floodgate had been opened. Although magazines had always offered frequency discounts and other incentives, there was a degree of equality and adherence to published rates. *McCall's* may have been the first, but discounting was an inevitability. Advertisers and agencies demanded further price cutting from all magazines, until the rate card virtually all but disappeared.

Today, virtually every magazine is forced to "go off rate card" either directly or by packaging "value-added" incentives into each buy. At a time when clients are seeking improved marketing support from media companies, the dynamics of the business have driven magazines into television-style commoditization and aggressive negotiation that minimizes direct involvement with the advertiser and centers sales efforts on the agency media buyer.

Conde Nast, publisher of *Vanity Fair, Glamour, Vogue* and several other leading magazines targeted to upscale audiences, has fought to maintain the integrity of its rate cards, losing business from major clients such as General Motors and Saks Fifth Avenue as a result. Conde Nast is among the most aggressive publishers in packaging value-added marketing programs in with media buys, effectively reducing page costs. This strategy is commendable, because it maintains a sense of priorities -- recognizing that the true value of a medium is its ability to support advertisers' marketing objectives. There are advertisers, however, such as General Motors, who believe that they can develop their own promotions and who clearly understand the role of media in the total marketing equation. For these advertisers, generating price concessions from media is necessary to fund their own promotional programs.

Therein lies the rub. If media allow themselves to become commodities, uninvolved in their clients' marketing processes, can they succeed or will promotional spending continue to eat up the media budget?

More and more, agency media buyers appear to be demanding both rate discounts *and* value-added merchandising deals from media companies. But the more commoditized the media industry becomes, the fewer revenues and profits the industry will have to meet its own long-term marketing needs. According to a study conducted in 1992 by Fairfield Research Inc. for *MediaWeek Magazine*, 91% of media sellers say that the demands by agencies for "value-added services" have increased in the past three years. Eighty-four percent believe that it will *not* be possible for media sellers to discontinue the added value incentives they are currently offering companies. Sixty-eight percent of media sellers, according to the Fairfield study, believe that advertising agencies and advertisers are more concerned with receiving rate cuts than with high quality media-buys.

But as long as there is more supply than there is demand, as exists in the media field, the deciding factor for media buyers will invariably be cost. If any medium is to successfully establish its unique value to the advertiser, it must relate that value back to its ability to motivate audiences to react in a certain way consistent with the advertiser's objectives. It is not sufficient to depend upon intuitive logic or unsupported claims of differentiation. Advertisers want to understand how a magazine's points of differentiation will translate into improved sales.

The increasing emphasis on magazines as commodities pushes magazine sales executives further away from their traditional role as marketing partners. Agency, advertiser and publishing executives share a common belief that the concept of "marketing support," which magazines have always provided, is on the decline just when it should be on the increase. Yet, economic realities are driving the business away from its traditional strengths.

‡

FROM COMMODITY TO MARKETING PARTNER

Today, advertisers are becoming increasingly interested in the potential of building new relationships with their media vendors, but they are also locked into traditional requirements that media purchases be as "cheap" as can possibly be negotiated. They are caught in the paradox of demanding the lowest prices for their media time and space while also being interested in how they can gain marketing benefits through enhanced knowledge of and involvement in the media decision-making processes. Much like the conversion in the insurance business from salespeople to "financial planners," in the advertising business, media salespeople must convert from a "lowest price negotiation" strategy and place increased emphasis on improving their services and marketing capabilities. Like the financial services industry, the media industry will ultimately undergo a successful restructuring to provide marketing services to its clients.

More than 75% of corporate marketing executives express a desire to be more directly involved on a person-to-person basis with their agency's media planners and media company representatives. The role of media in the success of an advertising campaign is increasingly perceived by clients as equal in importance to the creative product. Agency media planners and media sales reps, however, are not integrally involved in marketing planning and are rarely given direct responsibility for assuring that synergy exists between the media plan, overall marketing objectives and non-advertising promotional activities.

But the trend toward emphasizing long-term marketing applications of media has become pronounced in just the past year.

THE MEDIA RESPOND

In 1991 and 1992, CBS Television and Time Inc. Magazines radically restructured their sales organizations.

Time Inc. Magazines conducted a highly visible reorganization of its sales organization in 1991. Rather than individual sales representatives calling on agency media planners for each of the Time Inc. magazines, they created an umbrella sales organization that could represent the complete stable of Time publications (including *Time, Fortune, People, Entertainment Weekly, Money* and several others) to advertisers and agencies. The change was controversial, caused internal turmoil at Time, and power has ultimately returned to individual publishers. But Time was accurately anticipating and responding to a trend that others will successfully follow.

Advertising agency DMB&B's *Media Insights* newsletter reports that "ABC, CBS and NBC are starting to change the way they do business, questioning the validity of time honored rituals and icons like the fall premiere season, the upfront market, the household rating, the single standard of audience measurement and affiliate compensation. It's a good thing too. The faster they change, the better their odds of prospering in a fast changing environment."

CBS Television, under new sales management headed by Peter Lund, spent two years analyzing the advertiser and agency marketplace, conducting a major proprietary study to define industry trends and to determine if their existing selling structure was appropriate for the future.

The traditional structure had a separate selling force

representing each major daypart, typically Prime Time, Sports and News, Daytime, Late Night/Weekend. Each sales force was complemented by an independent daypart planning organization that set rates and managed inventory allocation for this daypart. This organization worked well in responding to the "Agency-of-Record" (AOR) structure of many national advertisers, which assigned their network spending by daypart to different agencies, according to that agency's particular skills and experience.

In effect, this AOR structure represented the first stage of media consolidation. While agencies maintained media planning responsibilities on their individual brands, advertisers consolidated the buying for all brands by daypart at each daypart agency-of-record.

In 1991, CBS determined that many clients were planning or initiating consolidation of their media spending. While they did not expect daypart AOR structuring to disappear, CBS decided it would be in the *advertisers'* best interests if CBS reorganized its sales department to create agency "team leaders" who represented all dayparts.

While there continues to be daypart experts at CBS and other networks, the reorganization reflected a recognition of the importance of identifying and serving the needs of the advertiser. While several network television "daypart buying experts" at large agencies, who individually control millions of dollars in specific network daypart budgets, consider the changes to work to their detriment, the shift toward a "client friendly" sales structure is irrevocable.

CBS was also accurate in recognizing the emergence of a trend away from daypart AOR's. While the trends of the past have approached the media buy as a sum of its parts, with each part handled independently by different media experts, the new trend is toward consolidation of all media under a single umbrella. By handling each medium independently, thus separating print from television, from outdoor, from yellow pages, from place-based media, the client and agency were minimizing the opportunities for media to work as a single entity toward a common set of objectives.

These changes at CBS were initially developed, but not implemented, as early as 1978. In 1978, as Director of Marketing for the CBS Television Stations division, I wrote a report identifying strategic issues for CBS management. "Technology," I wrote, "is being created at a pace faster than our industry can respond to it." As a result of that report, which accurately predicted the rapid ascent of cable television as a viable network competitor, Tom Leahy, then president of the CBS-TV stations division, approved an annual $2 million budget to "organize a long-term marketing and sales effort intended to strengthen the sales effort, build direct relationships with clients, attract new clients to television, and prepare for the changes in our business over the next ten years."

David Poltrack, who, as CBS' executive vice president, has become the leading researcher in the television industry, had preceded me in the CBS Stations' marketing job and had organized an excellent research and support organization for the stations. With slight restructuring, we had a new business development strike force that was a model for a client services marketing organization which would clearly establish CBS as a marketing leader well before it became popular in the 1990s.

In 1979 and 1980, the group was responsible for creating the explosion in jeans advertising. Working closely with Warren Hirsh, president of Murjani International, we launched Gloria Vanderbilt Jeans as a major television advertiser. Murjani's success was followed by that of Sasson and others. We then met and worked closely with Calvin Klein, John Weitz, Bill Blass and other top designers, making fashion the fastest growing category in television ad spending in the early 1980s.

However, in the early 1980s, CBS began a wrenching series of management shifts. John Backe was replaced by Tom Wyman as company president, which translated down the ranks into increased control by young financial turks, trained at Harvard and Wharton but with little practical broadcasting or sales experience. The emphasis was on stock market value and quarterly financial results.

Tom Leahy moved to the CBS Network and was replaced as stations division president by Neil Derrough, general manager of WCBS-TV in New York. Neil made several management changes, bringing in a new team of financial managers as his closest advisors.

Derrough decided that the investment in an independent business development/marketing team was unnecessary and that each station should be responsible for its own efforts. The team was dismantled after being in existence for only two years and generating nearly three million dollars in new business. Derrough's decision was based on common thinking in the broadcast and advertising industry in 1981. Focusing on direct client selling and new business development in the broadcasting industry was akin to Columbus saying the world was round, and the response about as supportive. Warnings about the impending growth of cable drew derisive comparisons to Chicken Little. Marketing, it was thought, was an inefficient waste of shareholders' money.

DO YOU KNOW YOUR SISTER?

In 1981, a plan was also presented to senior CBS management outlining a corporate sales department that would be responsible for packaging all CBS properties, which at the time included the television and radio networks, several television and radio stations in major markets, Columbia Records, a publishing empire incorporating consumer and trade magazines, a large book publishing company, and several other businesses. The idea is one that several major media companies are today attempting to follow, but in 1981 concerns about anti-trust regulations prevented direct divisional interaction.

Media companies have avoided offering corporate packages because many fear the result will be forced discounting. It also reflects patterns established in the 1960s and 1970s when governmental anti-trust actions forced CBS to sell its program development arm (it was spun off to create Viacom, which today owns MTV, Nickelodeon and Showtime) and ABC to divest itself of its theatrical distribution business.

Today, media companies are recognizing the obvious value of integrating their capabilities -- of pulling together the resources of sister companies. While costs-per-thousand continue to be a primary measure of competitive comparison, they do not speak to the *effectiveness* of a medium or group of media in meeting advertisers' objectives and sales goals. Cost-per-thousand does not define for advertisers what is and is not working. Media companies must aggressively seek to develop relationships with advertisers that identify opportunities for meeting marketing goals and objectives -- for selling products and services. As Peter Spengler, vice president of marketing for Bristol-Myers Squibb Company, points out: "There's too much emphasis on the deal and not enough on its value."

Television or radio program ratings and magazine or newspaper circulation do not tell us if a media buy is good or bad. While most media planners and agency media departments work very diligently to be creative in their decision-making, the reality of today's business environment is that the effectiveness of these executives is measured by how well they drive media costs downward.

Television and radio ratings and magazine and newspaper circulation figures only tell us how many people are exposed to a publication. Media buyers are increasingly measured by how effectively they negotiate for lower costs-per-thousand. As a result, there is little motivation among agencies to seek marketing synergies from media companies.

A television media sales person at Fox Television may have received a multi-million dollar order from the agency for a Procter & Gamble product with no awareness at any level within the corporation that *TV Guide* or *Mirabella* Magazine, also owned by Fox parent News Corporation, received a major piece of P&G business. Furthermore, P&G most likely is purchasing free standing coupon inserts from News America, the FSI arm of News Corp.

While News Corp. and other companies such as Time-Warner have sought to develop corporate selling groups, the reality is that the structure of the media buying and selling system defeats such efforts. For these efforts to succeed in the future, the Knowledge Resources Manager's emphasis on media and agency capabilities and resources must be implemented. Just as the advertising agency requires individuals who are immersed in the advertisers' marketing objectives, media companies must also install in positions of leadership executives who interface directly with advertisers and who have strong marketing skills and experience. A media company's marketing director should work with the agency's Knowledge Resources Manager and the advertiser to pull together all the media company's resources to fulfill the advertiser's goals and objectives.

No matter what their titles, individuals who are charged with the responsibility for identifying and maximizing the effectiveness of available marketing, advertising, promotional and media resources will increasingly dominate the advertising business. Those companies that hire and empower these executives will survive the attacks on advertising and be the major power brokers in the next millenium.

!

PART 5

GETTING A JOB,
KEEPING A JOB,
AND GETTING PROMOTED

THE LOTTERY TICKET SOCIETY

We live in a lottery ticket society. Too many of us believe that we can only achieve wealth through luck, not through hard work or a great idea. To a large degree, our culture has glorified talent as something that very few members of society have, and that without it, we cannot expect to achieve great success. Athletes, musicians, actors... these are the stars that society is rewarding.

Do we fear that success in real life is too distant a goal to seek? Is ambition today no more than tilting at windmills? The trend forecasters of the 1970s predicted that in the year 2000, the average worker would have a four-day, 32-hour work week. Leisure time activities would represent the fastest-growing business category.

Every person I know is working harder today than ever before, and there are no indications this will change in the near or distant future. We are working harder, with little assurance that we're getting ahead. We're running harder and faster, but the wind blowing in our faces is pushing us further and further back. Between 1969 and 1989, median family income in constant dollars rose only $562, from $28,344 to $28,906, according to Bill McKibben, author of *The Age of Missing Information*.

I began this book by writing about the shift to a more linear society, in which we have little sense of patterns and continuity -- of beginnings, middles and ends. Careers are much the same.

In an early episode of the classic television program *Life with Father,* daughter Betty announced that she intended to grow up an be an engineer. Mother and Father ignored her, laughing off this "female folly." We know today, of course, that Betty certainly could have succeeded in her ambition, and no program that scoffed at this dream would ever clear network programmers.

Our greatest strength as a society has been our belief in better things to come, supported and reinforced by our media and our advertising. The future, we have always believed, holds promise. Careers can begin in the mailroom and wind up in the corporate boardroom. *We paid dues.* My dues included traveling once a week to Brooklyn, selling bus advertising, and investing all my savings to start a business. But I believed, without question, that careers moved inevitably forward.

Today, I meet many young people who are less willing to pay dues. Careers, they believe, are like movies or plays; they expect a smash hit right from the very beginning. The excesses in the financial community during the 1980s, when young stock brokers moved immediately into six figure salaries, are similar to the excesses in the media and advertising communities. Young media sales people and creative hotshots are making $100,000 plus incomes before they hit 30 years old. Their ambition to move into management and their understanding of the industries in which they work are frightfully lacking.

Recently, a baseball superstar was introduced to the wife of baseball legend Lou Gehrig. Oblivious to Gehrig's name and status as one of baseball's greatest players, and wondering why Mrs. Gehrig was in the clubhouse, the superstar asked if the lady's grandson was a player. Similarly, advertising, media and marketing executives often become hugely successful before they are adequately steeped in "the game." For several of my clients, I test their employees with simple questions about their own business. For media organizations, I ask about their programming or editorial product and that of their competitors. I ask television station sales executives about the anchors on their station's 6:30 AM newscast, or what is on at 10:30 AM, 2:30 AM, or even Wednesday at 8:30 PM. I'll ask company brand managers about the various media in which their advertising runs, and I'll ask agency media executives about a broad cross-section of media and creative issues.

The average score, on a 100 point scale, is under 50%! Worse, few younger executives are steeped in the history of the industry. They have never read the books of David Ogilvy or Jerry Della Femina. They do not understand the influence of Fairfax Cone, Raymond Rubicam, Ted Bates, Herbert Krugman, Bill Bernbach, or the great early publishers and television pioneers. They have no idea that Sigourney Weaver's father, Sylvester (Pat) Weaver, was responsible for creating the *Today* and *Tonight* shows. When they watch *20/20*, they're unaware of the contribution Hugh Downs has made to the television industry or the role of Barbara Walters in shattering the glass ceiling for female newscasters.

Many young advertising, media and marketing executives believe that it is culturally unacceptable to be a creature of media. I'm still amazed that so many young interviewees thought it was appropriate to tell the CBS Television executive, with whom they were interviewing, that they watched "very little television."

Success in the advertising industry -- any facet of it -- should require being a student of the business. It should be required that ad agency media executives *consume* media -- television, magazines, newspapers, in-store, etc. How else can they relate to and understand opportunities when they are presented? How else can they develop and implement creative applications of media with an instinctive foundation of knowledge about what will work and what won't?

As in society, careers in the advertising, marketing and media fields are becoming "have" and "have-not" careers, and the delineation between the successful and the unsuccessful is too often the ability to generate short-term revenue gains. Vision, knowledge and attention to long-term relationships are rarely rewarded. Too many young people "make it" within their first few years in the business and have little preparation for the positions of higher authority into which they are placed. While they may be more willing to take risks than the more conservative older generation of management, they are not adequately prepared to differentiate reasonable from unreasonable risks.

They have been trained to focus on immediate results, with little understanding of the long-term impact or repercussions of their decisions. Brand managers in many companies are charged with the responsibility for increasing sales of their brands. Success, they know, will drive them upward into management ranks or out into a better position at a better company.

Their promotions depend not on how effectively they position their brands for the future, but whether or not their year-to-year sales improved *each month*.

Advertising agency creative executives too often measure their own careers by the awards they win, and their ability to convert those awards into bigger salaries. Media buying executives are evaluated by their negotiating prowess, and by their ability to generate maximum audience exposure within specific budgets. Few awards are given for media creativity, and those that are given rarely translate into industry stardom. Account executives are rewarded for keeping clients satisfied, and for maintaining agency accounts with minimum loss. Yet, we read of account executives and creative executives leaving agencies *with their clients.* Loyalty has become a commodity to be sold to the highest bidder.

Media salespeople move up the ranks quickly. The average salesperson at a local mid to large market television station earns more than $70,000, and many network and magazines sales executives are compensated well into the six figures.

These executives work hard for their success, and their compensation for this work should not be criticized. But, in many instances, it's too much too soon, and it is not accompanied by the proper training and preparation for a long career.

Relationships between employees and their companies, and between companies and their clients are increasingly short-lived. Positions are jobs, rather than careers. Myers Reports mails thousands of letters each year to ad executives. In 1992, more than 20% of our correspondence was returned. Attrition. Moves. Firings. Lay-offs. Recession. *Change.*

The Japanese have created a system of loyalties in business built upon "Dokikai." As new groups of employees enter a company, they form fast friendships that continue throughout their careers. Whether an employee has become company president or stayed in the entry level position, members of the "dokikai" are obligated to state "honto" to each other -- their true feelings on any business subject.

In this country, our driving ambition to succeed often causes us to state "tatemae," saying what is expected, rather than "honto." Employees rapidly moving from one company to another, and intense pressure for promotions within companies virtually assure that few employees feel free to state what is truly on their mind for fear that their feelings are not consistent with their management's objectives.

As we mature in our careers, we form "dokikai" with a few, very select friends and associates whom we have learned to trust. Typically, these individuals are not within our own companies and they serve as advisors, rather than forces for moving a business. The adversarial foundations of the advertising, marketing and media businesses have encouraged career-minded individuals to think only in linear patterns -- like digital clocks moving ahead with no sense of continuity.

Our business focus should be on preparing for the person who will follow us after we move into another position. The role of every individual should be to take responsibility for clearly demonstrating how his or her job *function* is being enhanced and how it is enhancing the process of which it is a part. We should not only be concerned with the progress of one's individual career. Deming's principles of *Total Quality Management* should become the measure of every employee's success. Total Quality Management requires that every job task be performed slightly better each time it is performed, with commitment to improvement.

The future of the marketing, advertising and media businesses depends upon improved training programs and expanded emphasis on "honto." Relationships are the key to the future. An essential tool for career success is sharing your true feelings *on every business subject. We should demand of ourselves, and those upon whom we depend for advice and counsel, that we be experts in our business, with a perspective on the past and a vision for the future. Knowledge and experience are the keys to career success.*

Each year thousands of graduates pour out of the nation's colleges and universities. If America's greatness once was manifest in the dreams of its young, its current economic conditions now have imposed a more austere reality. Today, the hopes and dreams of college students simply are for a meaningful entry level job. They are moving back into their parents' homes and are being forced to accept jobs far afield from their hopes and aspirations. For my readers who are well into their careers, skip to page 271. The next pages are for readers who are in their career's formative years.

First, do not despair. Success in the 1990s and beyond will come to those who perserver. For those who have made it this far through *Adbashing,* the career opportunities of the future should be obvious. Start at your local cable television system in any capacity -- as an advertising sales assistant or production assistant. Become an outbound telemarketing operator, learning the direct sales business from the bottom up. (This is a great part-time opportunity during college years.) Investigate opportunities at the weekly shopper. Search out a local ad agency that has interesting retail accounts, and offer to serve as an low paid -- or even unpaid -- intern working on those accounts. Why retail? Because you can implement innovative ideas based upon impact and frequency and generate measurable results.

Take advantage of your summers during college by working in the ad business as an unpaid or low-paid intern. Many companies hire their interns once they graduate. Work at a company where you'll have the opportunity to build relationships with several executives and with clients or vendors. Use the college years to build a resume and relationships, which will serve you better than your degree in your hunt for a job.

Upon accepting an internship, agree to do meaningful, relevant work for little or no pay, but also ask that your employer pay you if you do clerical-type work. No work is meaningless, and you'll be a more valuable employee when you help with the overload of day-to-day tasks. But keep a record of this work and submit a weekly invoice to your employer.

Once you have a job, learn and absorb as much as possible. But also bring a fresh perspective to your responsibilities, unfettered by traditions and past experience. Most importantly, speak your mind. Do not hesitate to challenge the establishment. Change is inevitable. The MTV generation that can relate to the 500 channel environment is far more qualified to develop successful advertising strategies in the 1990s than the "age wave" generation.

Consume media. When you're in the business, your magazine and newspaper subscriptions and your cable hook-ups are tax deductible. Spend as much time as possible watching, reading and trying to spot opportunities and trends. Start reading the advertising and marketing trade publications early in your career. *ADWEEK, Advertising Age, MediaWeek, BRANDWEEK, Inside Media, Magazine Week, Broadcasting, Cable Avails, Multichannel News, Cablevision* -- these are the trade publications that you should be reading from college until retirement. Reading the trades plus the *Wall Street Journal, New York Times, USA Today* and your local newspaper keep you one step ahead of your competitors.

We used to say (and most people still do) that it's a "dog eat dog" world. I don't agree. It's a world where those who are smarter and more aggressive get ahead, but the political infighter who "stabs others in the back" is no longer a welcome individual in most corporations. Corporations can only succeed when their employees are watching each others' backs from outside competition and aggression. There is no time or place for internal struggles and battles. Certainly they occur. In any organization, large or small, politics is inevitable. But those who invest too much of their time and energy on the affairs of others will ultimately lose. President Clinton's campaign avoided attacks on his opponents, while the Bush campaign machine embraced the politics of the '80s. Like George Bush, employees who engage in negative and hostile behavior will ultimately fail. Avoid company gossip and "think up." Even as a junior employee, emulate in dress and behavior those senior managers whom you respect. This doesn't mean you should avoid social activities, but practice moderation. Drink in moderation; don't *ever* get drunk with co-workers; don't smoke; and avoid sexual relationships. Be social; participate in company events; use these opportunities to meet others and extend your relationships.

Most importantly, *build* relationships. Take every opportunity to meet new people. Follow up on meetings with notes of thanks; send relevant news clippings with a short personal letter; call to set another meeting or lunch. Be sure to come with information, ideas, or news. Never schedule a meeting without a fresh idea that refers to your contact's expressed needs and interests. Never hesitate to ask in-depth probing questions about someone's business. You'll be surprised how much you can learn.

Ultimately, success depends upon ambition, assertiveness, creativity and initiative. Success is built on a foundation of relationships, perceptions, ideas, experiences and skill. And it is built one step at a time. The most important step, the most difficult, is the first one. Work on an effective resume.

Personalize a cover letter that demonstrates what you know about a company. And don't offer "references upon request." If you have good references, put them right up front. Use whatever relationships you have to get in the door. Identify a company for which you want to work and be relentless. Pursue. Remember the basic rules of frequency. Don't let up.

Once you have that first job, be prepared to follow your career path wherever it may take you. Watch for opportunities. If you become convinced you're on the wrong path, don't just jump off. Unemployment is not the most effective reference. I've never agreed with the philosophy of leaving one job to have the time to look for another. It sounds stupid. It sounds like you've been fired. If you are fired, it's only a setback -- not a defeat. It's a red badge of courage. Understand the reasons and avoid them in the future.

I believe that hard work pays off. Come in early. Go home late. Spend time with others in the organization to learn about their jobs and responsibilities. If your immediate supervisor or his/her boss is working late, offer to help out. Ask to learn about other areas of the company. Take on as much responsibility as possible. Ask your supervisor to assess your performance and offer recommendations on how you can improve your work. Employers must give you fair warning of any deficiencies in your performance before you can be terminated with cause. If you've been advised of problems, ask each week if you're improving. Your supervisor must give you specific advice on what you need to do to improve your performance. If it's clear that there's a problem that won't go away, get out before it hits the fan. Start looking for a job.

Don't hesitate to ask for a raise when it's due. Unless you're working for an employer with structured pay scales and annual increases, you'll most likely get a raise only when you ask for it. I've always respected those who respect their own value and who expect to be paid for their efforts. Finally, understand your own ambitions. Some people enjoy small cities and companies; others believe they've only made it when they've made it in New York, L.A. or Chicago.

There is no right or wrong. Stay where you are most comfortable both geographically and organizationally. Some people are entrepreneurial; some are ambitious. Some of the best salespeople I've known have made terrible managers, and vice versa. If you've been promoted into a job or area that just doesn't work for you, it won't work for the company either. It's not dishonorable to recognize where your contribution can be most valuable.

Success in today's business environment demands total commitment, thorough planning and complete confidence in your own capabilities and those upon whom you depend. Experience and hands-on involvement are essential components of winning game plans. The dynamic of mind-catching creative ideas -- powerfully delivered -- is the foundation of successful marketing. Beyond simply creative ideas, promotion must generate a reaction. It must sell the ideas. Successful marketing is tactically focused on today's business needs within a strategic vision of tomorrow's opportunities. Your success will be inevitable when you organize the forces of imagination, planning, knowledge, involvement and effort.

❡

PART 6

❢

ALVIN TOFFLER, WOODY ALLEN AND THE TITANIC

CHANGE AND THRIVE

In *Power Shift,* Alvin Toffler identifies knowledge as the "crux of tomorrow's worldwide struggle for power," replacing the clout of money. "The basic flaw in the old strategies," Toffler points out, "is that they still focus on the circulation and clout of money instead of knowledge."

The same can be said of the marketing, advertising and media businesses. There is a great deal of confusion about the future of advertising and media. Marketers' increasing dependence upon promotional activities has caused a radical decline in their dependence upon traditional advertising and media. With that has come a dramatic increase in the supply of media options. Executives are paid extremely well to meet immediate revenue goals, but few have a clear vision of their long-term future.

Some suggest that the advertising business is in crisis. The Chinese word for crisis is composed of two characters: one for danger and the other for opportunity. Woody Allen described the situation that some of my colleagues believe we are now in:

"We are at a crossroads. One path leads to extinction and the other to utter despair. Let's hope we're wise enough to take the right path."

There is a third option, and it lies in the word "opportunity." By thinking our only paths are to extinction or utter despair, we are admitting that we, as an industry, cannot and will not change.

As I've demonstrated throughout this book, change is happening all around us: at the most traditional of companies like CBS, BBDO and Time-Warner; at newer companies like Turner Broadcasting, K-III Magazines and Whittle Communications; and at the hundreds of entrepreneurial companies like Myers Reports, Ammirati & Puris, Marketing Resources Plus and Liberty Media. All of our experiences of the past 100 years in the advertising and media businesses have conspired to make too many of us resistent to change. The fear of change is our most dangerous enemy in business today. We have had the warnings and the opportunities. More than ten years ago, in the March, 1981 issue of *Marketing & Media Decisions* Magazine, James Walsh, then the advertising manager for Merrill Lynch, wrote:

"The people who run the nation's media should consider moving 'Innovative Marketing' up on their list of priorities. Right now it seems to reside in about tenth place, well below sales, distribution, programing, ratings, circulation. But they probably won't do it. The attitude seems to be 'why change a good thing.' We're in the TV business or the publications business and we know our business very well."

Walsh went on to call for "a lot of thought, hard work, creativity and *a genuine concern for the advertiser's needs.*"

The erosion of advertising's share of marketing budgets and the comparatively low esteem in which media is held by marketers attests to the lack of response to Walsh's call to action. In the past, competing interests among media companies restricted us from looking even for those few areas where common interests permitted limited cooperation.

Today, the growing number of common values and a shared need to generate sales results for marketers have created almost limitless possibilities for developing cooperative projects that serve mutual interests. Marketers increasingly will select their advertising agencies and media *partners* on the basis of these companies' commitment to change and their ability to bring new ideas and new knowledge to the decision-making process.

It would be a fundamental error for those who have the opportunity to change to think that there is no better alternative to the present. One hundred years of the existing advertising and media buying and selling structure has instilled a pervasive egalitarian ethic and a resistance to change in our business. But real and enduring growth for the advertising and media industries can result only from a recognition of the need to respond to crisis by facing the dangers, taking the risks, and changing the very foundations upon which the industry has been built.

The crisis faced today in the advertising business is not driven by declining margins and shrinking profitability. Rather, it is caused by executives who respond tactically to these problems in an effort to build a more cost-effective structure instead of approaching their business with a visionary, strategic sense of the future.

Executives are charged with the responsibility of being businesspersons, but very few are building their businesses; they are trying to build more cost-effective entities rather than building bridges to more profitable opportunities. Every effort, every risk taken, no matter how large or small, should be viewed as a step forward and applauded. One agency executive accused a major media company that was changing its organizational structure of "taking half-measures, of rearranging deck chairs on the Titanic." The media industry, he said, "is sinking." This agency executive, rather than seeking opportunities, was subscribing to the Woody

Allen philosophy of extinction or utter despair.

It is more important that we support half-measures and small risks, so that they may become full efforts and be more certain of success. It is incumbent upon all executives in our business that we embrace change.

The issues for the future that we must address are the basic structural foundations that support advertising as a marketing tool and as a profession. Can we shift from a measurement base dependent upon cost efficiency to one based upon effectiveness in meeting corporate marketing objectives?

Can we convert advertising to an accountability system based upon the bottom line rather than the bottom price? Will media traditionalists recognize the holy grail of frequency, and begin organizing their media purchases based upon completely new patterns of advertising placement and distribution?

Is the media industry receptive to forming new relationships and rebuilding sales organizations to respond to changes in how and why decisions are made and who is making them? Is the industry able to gain a perspective on its past and move sufficiently away from that past to gain a vision of the future?

The ball is in your court - every reader has the opportunity to respond. The casual reader who simply enjoys watching television should recognize and support those marketers and media who seek to communicate with you in new and direct ways. Do not accept the vocal pleas of activists and regulators who would diminish the role of advertising and the expansive choice of media it underwrites.

Professionals in the marketing, advertising and media

businesses can seek new opportunities to form more meaningful relationships with each other. Success in the future will be increasingly relational. In the past, companies often mouthed the rhetoric of partnership. In the future, companies will be thrust into it. They must embrace new relationships if they are to succeed and grow. Marketers, advertising agencies and media companies will be increasingly linked to one another, dependent upon each other for the knowledge they require to accomplish their single objective: sales results for the marketer.

The path taken by marketing, advertising and media executives is a critical one. Our economy and our worldwide success has been built based upon the historic leadership and success of the United States as a marketing and communications force. As a single industry, we have a responsibility to assure that our media choices continue to receive the necessary funding to expand worldwide and thrive financially. To achieve that end, their primary source of funding -- advertising -- must continue to be perceived as a viable, valuable marketing tool that is not subjected to censorship or taxation. The future of the advertising and media businesses is dependent upon the changes we make and the risks we take today.

We, as an industry, must recognize that adbashing is a threat to capitalism, to a free press, to our basic forms of entertainment, and to the future of our children. To survive the attacks on advertising, we must respond.

We must change.

❧

JACK MYERS'

MEDIA MEGATRENDS

MYERS REPORTS
WORLDWIDE
Marketing Leadership Panel

MEGATREND ONE:

MASS REACH MEDIA

ARE THE CROWN JEWELS

During the past 15 years, the share of the total marketing communications pie captured by traditional advertising media (television, radio, magazines, newspapers, out-of-home) has declined from 65% to approximately 22%. This share decline has paralleled the erosion of broadcast network's share of the television viewing pie from over 80% to 62% and the decline of the average three-network primetime audience share from 87% in 1979-80 to 60% in 1990-91.

The strength of advertising is brand equity building. But throughout the 1970s and 1980s, marketers emphasized short-term promotional efforts at the expense of brand building. The buying of media time and space became commodity based. Research and pricing focused upon quantitative evidence of audience size and composition. The advertising industry became inner-directed, oblivious to the erosion of its foundation. Research has not been developed to prove the value of advertising for building brand loyalty. As advertisers have become increasingly dissatisfied with their inability to measure the return on their media investments, their investments in brand-building advertising have declined. For short-term sales, they perceive advertising to compare unfavorably to trade promotion, consumer sales promotion and direct marketing.

There are only two solutions for the advertising industry. One: enhance the perceived value of advertising as a vehicle for increasing product distribution and generating short-term sales. Two: develop research tools that allow marketers to measure the direct correlation between advertising investments and brand awareness/perceptions.

As marketers recommit in the 1990s to establishing and maintaining brand loyalty (see Megatrend Two), the advertising industry must become more responsive to their needs. Advertisers believe that their most important advertising vehicle for establishing and maintaining brand loyalty has been broadcast network television, complemented by magazines and, more recently, by cable television. Brands that depend upon consumer loyalty fear continued erosion and fragmentation of television and magazine audiences. As much as they may support and even demand lower advertising costs that result from increased media supply and competition, they require the concentrations of audience reach that broadcast networks and magazines have historically provided.

Leading national advertisers tell us that broadcast networks are the engines that drive their advertising train. Without a solid foundation of mass reach media, advertising, as an industry, will continue to lose market share to direct marketing and promotion. The engine is sputtering, and if it cannot gain steam, the train may derail. The broadcast network business is unprofitable; it has become apparent that structural change in the advertising business is essential before network ratings and share erosion can be reversed. Increased competition from prime time syndication, affiliate preemptions, unwired networks and cable continue to fragment audiences.

Broadcast television networks are locked into the entertainment business, which is a "hit" business. Through the network/

studio relationship, multiple program concepts are developed, funded through the pilot process, and either discarded or accepted. Upwards of 10% of a network's development budget may be used for "pilot abandonment" -- programs that never see the light of day. Of those accepted as network series, two out of every ten historically survive and become profitable hits. These hits underwrite the deficits generated by the other eight "losers."

Today, the hit ratio is moving closer to one out of every ten programs. Compounding this problem is the reality that syndication revenues are declining and foreign distributors are purchasing fewer American programs. The profits generated by hits are not covering the deficits of all the losers.

For broadcast networks to increase profits:

-- costs must be reduced,

-- program quality and promotional efforts must be maintained and improved to attract larger audiences,

-- network revenues must be increased while cost-per-thousand efficiencies to advertisers are decreased.

New structures and relationships will be developed between advertisers and networks that support and reinforce networks' efforts to reduce costs while maintaining quality. Television Production Partners Inc. is developing a consortium of major national advertisers to support the broadcast networks' efforts to rebuild their profitability. TPP provides funding resources for 26-week program continuity, development of non-controversial high quality programming, elimination of pilots, creative multi-airing arrangements, and innovative approaches to cost reduction.

The three broadcast networks (four if Fox is included) recognize the value of marketing themselves as a single entity to the advertising community. The relationships established through the Network Television Association will extend to marketing/promotional projects and advertiser services as well. Marketers will also support magazine industry programs that enhance advertiser services while reducing costs.

Media companies will increasingly understand and accept their dependence upon a strong broadcast network marketplace supported by a multiplex of viable targeted media vehicles. The media industry will be forced to cease its destructive internecine warfare, understanding that all media must work together to grow *advertising's* share of the marketing pie.

Advertising in the 1990s is a new business, substantially different from the business of the 1980s or 1970s. The advertising forest has been full of foxes, rabbits, deer and wolves, all feeding on a plentiful bounty. Although they've attacked each other, all the species have survived. But there have been bears hiding in the woods -- promotion and direct marketing bears. These bears have been slowly and quietly eating up most of the vegetation and are now about to take over the forest, destroying the other life forms.

The deer, foxes, wolves and rabbits must combine their resources to fight back against the bears. They can no longer fight each other, for if they do, they are the unwitting accomplices of the bears. They must become partners, reinforcing their defenses and organizing their resources behind their strongest media weapons. The promotion and direct marketing bears must be driven back into their corners of the forest if the advertising industry is to survive and grow.

A megatrend for the 1990s and beyond:

Advertising industry and media trade associations will combine their resources to re-invent the advertising business with a new understanding that the industry must gather all its resources to compete effectively and with knowledge that, to paraphrase Pogo: "We have met the enemy and it is *not* us."

MEGATREND TWO:

BRAND LOYALTY

Throughout the 1980s, the advertising and media industries were blinded to their loss of share by the growing size of ad budgets invested to support the influx of new products, services and companies.

The number of automobile brands grew from 18 in 1975 to more than 40 in 1992, with multiple sub-brands within each product group. Rather than three-four major shampoo brands in 1970 (Breck and Prell controlled over 50% of the market), today there are over 100 brands, including generics. The ad budgets invested in the launch and growth of new products has been the goose, laying thousands of golden eggs for media companies and advertising agencies. *In the 1990s, the goose has died.*

Manufacturers are now consolidating brands and shrinking their brand base to support their core products -- those that are strong and profitable. There are fewer product introductions. New products that do come to market receive less media support. Marketers are dependent upon trade promotion, direct marketing and consumer sales promotion for the bulk of their marketing activities.

As an industry, advertising must focus on how it can enhance marketers' ability to establish and maintain brand loyalty. Secondly, traditional media must offer integrated direct marketing and promotional capabilities as a basic component of their business. Thirdly, the ad industry must develop the measurements to prove the effectiveness of advertising for generating sales *and* establishing brand loyalty.

If the ad industry fails to achieve these goals, corporate investments in advertising will decline at a precipitous rate during the next five-seven years. As total marketing budgets decline, the advertising industry *must* capture a larger share of existing budgets. Advertising industry growth can no longer depend upon new product introductions. In the era of product consolidation, media must stem and reverse the erosion of its share of total marketing investments.

The advertising industry must re-orient its priorities and understand how, as an industry, it can best compete with promotion and direct marketing. It is not practical to denigrate these services. Advertising should attack only from a position of strength. Established brand equity is a valuable commodity as mega-retailers Kmart, Wal-mart and others allocate more shelf-space to unbranded "generic" products. Only high demand branded products will control their own distribution destiny. Advertising, as an industry, must focus on its ability to create, build and maintain awareness and loyalty for branded products and services, clearly demonstrating, through research, the value of advertising for creating consumer demand and driving retail distribution.

More important than a presentation of *why* advertising works to build brand identity is *how* it works. Media companies must fund research to identify the core advertising processes that achieve marketers' specific objectives. This research should be conducted in partnership between media companies and major marketers to establish proprietary knowledge, enabling marketers to refine their media use based upon actual results.

Integrated marketing, which combines advertising with sales promotion, direct marketing and other marketing capabilities, has not proven to be a practical reality for advertising agencies. Ad agencies attempting to absorb promotion and direct marketing is much like the goldfish trying to swallow the shark. Conversely, promotion agencies and organizations such as Michael Ovitz's Creative Artists Agency pose a threat to the ad agency business. They are positioned to absorb the traditional roles of the ad agency by operating as full marketing partners for their clients and, piece by piece, embracing the advertising agency's traditional responsibilities.

Sales promotion, trade promotion and advertising serve three different and distinct functions. In this context, media and ad agencies can slowly incorporate consumer sales promotion and direct marketing budgets into advertising budgets by demonstrating how advertising can support a consumer sales promotion effort. To succeed, *media companies* should integrate consumer sales promotion, direct marketing and research services into their capabilities, providing marketers with turn-key programs that:
-- establish brand identity;
-- drive sell-through at retail by providing promotional reinforcement and motivation;
-- and measure results in both areas.

A new foundation of strength for the advertising industry will be built upon building brand equity for marketers and drawing revenues from trade promotion budgets into integrated advertising/sales promotion programs.

Brand loyalty is the pillar that holds up traditional advertising media. The advertising industry's attack on its competition must focus on:

-- renewed commitment among marketers to building consumer brand awareness and loyalty;

-- rebuilt confidence in the contribution of advertising to brand equity building;

-- research that clearly demonstrates *how* advertising builds brand awareness and loyalty;

-- integration of consumer sales promotion and direct marketing capabilities into advertising campaigns to join brand advertising with directly measurable short-term sales results;

-- recognition among media companies and trade associations that the competitive opportunity is to draw budgets away from trade promotion to integrated advertising/promotion campaigns.

MEGATREND THREE:

COST REDUCTION

It's called value. Marketers have lost their sense of advertising and media value. It will be rediscovered in the 1990s.

The drive toward increased media commoditization, which has reduced the cost basis of most major media in the past few years, is more than a cost-reduction strategy by advertisers. Rather, it represents a dramatic restructuring of their priorities. As advertising has accounted for a smaller percentage of their total spending, marketers have systematically focused on those media that offer the greatest cost efficiencies, with little reluctance to walk away from those media and/or companies that are least efficient.

Marketers have demonstrated a willingness to eliminate any media company or medium from their marketing plans, *or even to walk away from advertising altogether* if necessary.

Those media companies that believe a renewed economy will send their rate cards shooting up are in a for a shock. The most successful media companies will be those that identify and develop new and innovative opportunities to increase their value to advertisers *at lower costs.* Advertisers want quality; they will support media that invest in building stronger relationships with their audiences. But advertisers have also made it very clear that they consider media costs to be too high. *Media cannot expect to fund enhanced capabilities and services through increased costs.* Advertisers want to have their cake and eat it too. They require enhanced services at *reduced* costs.

The United States, to reduce the deficit and avoid inflation, must operate government at dramatically reduced costs while increasing services to both its populace and the world. While doing this, it must fund a superstructure and marketing programs that enable American corporations to compete on quality with the Pacific Rim and European nations.

This demands improved efficiencies. Funding of a business, like our nation, can no longer depend solely on increased revenues. *Operating costs must be reduced. Salaries must be brought into line. Underperforming employees can no longer be supported.* The concepts of unemployment and welfare reflect a society that accepts and tolerates lack of performance. Business is the funding mechanism that supports the population. Government, in affect, must support business so that business can support its citizens. Yet, business is restricted and even repressed by our government. Government should get *into* aggressive support of corporations that create employment for the underprivileged, minorities, elderly, etc. The goal of government is full employment, which can be accomplished by reducing the dependence of able workers on the government for their financial support.

I've introduced this political statement to reinforce that advertisers, for their own survival, will inevitably cease their funding of those media vehicles that are no longer measurably productive for them. Marketers will no longer support those media that are not effective *and efficient*. The fragmentation of advertising budgets, which escalated throughout the 1980s, is reversing itself. While fiber optics, digital compression, satellite distribution and other technologies suggest continued fragmentation of television media, advertisers are no longer willing to fund these advances.

Marketers currently have available to them relatively effective and efficient vehicles for promotional and direct marketing activities. While interactive technologies may enhance these capabilities in television, they are accompanied by a high price tag. Television programmers may envision the appeal of a 500 channel universe, but the willingness of consumers and advertisers to fund these channels is doubtful.

Magazines, newspapers and cable television are primarily dependent upon a dual revenue stream: advertisers and subscribers. If mass media disappear, replaced instead by myriad low rated, small circulation vehicles, advertising revenues will most certainly decline. Messages can be distributed to small groups via direct marketing and promotional efforts more efficiently and effectively than print or television media. The success and growth of small circulation television vehicles and magazines are driven by the broad awareness-building capabilities of their mass circulation counterparts.

Unless overall media value is increased, advertisers will continue to withdraw support from advertising, as they have for every year since 1975. If advertisers are not willing to pay increased costs, then media companies must find new ways to reduce their overhead while increasing quality and services. Every citizen of the media community -- every television and radio program, every magazine, every newspaper section, every billboard -- must operate at a profit. Losses at any level, except in an investment mode, cannot be tolerated. The media business must emphasize cost management, in order to reduce costs to advertisers while increasing audience size and loyalty.

The future belongs to those companies and individuals that seek and find new and innovative ways to reduce their costs while increasing their quality and their profits. Just as major marketers are developing every-day-low-cost strategies in a basic restructuring of their business philosophies, so must the media industry respond to advertisers' needs for assurances of media efficiency.

MEGATREND FOUR:

MEDIA: THE ASCENDING STAR

Creativity. In the advertising business, creativity i associated with the messages that appear in print, video or audio Agencies have a "creative" department, but media departments don' have "creative" divisions. Media is a service department withir advertising agencies. While creativity in media planning i: welcomed, the media selection process is done primarily *by the numbers*.

As marketers demand that their advertising be accountable, media creativity will become a necessity to convert media plans from quantitatively measurable to qualitatively responsible. Successful media plans can no longer be measured strictly by the numbers. Brands will be differentiated through their media selection and usage. New media opportunities, as identified in *Adbashing: Surviving the Attacks on Advertising*, will be pursued. Those media executives and organizations that are responsive to their clients' *marketing* needs and deliver effective, as well as efficient, media buys will ascend to stardom both within their organizations and within the industry.

As advertising agencies "unbundle" their media departments to increase their profitability, it will be necessary for these unbundled organizations to competitively differentiate themselves. The ultimate creation of a core group of mega-media organizations will shift the emphasis from cost efficiency to planning and buying creativity. Advertisers will quickly appreciate that any one of several alternative buying groups will provide the lowest available pricing.

Once this is realized, advertisers will look to other issues to determine the media buying/planning organization that offers the most advantageous services. These services include compensation, administrative simplicity, computerization, marketing capabilities, media planning and creative media applications. Other than the latter, each of these services is tenuous and transitory, as one organization matches the services of the others.

The primary differentiation will be in the creativity of personnel and management. Negotiating skills, which are a primary selling point of media buying organizations today, will become less meaningful as media costs decline. Advertisers will look instead toward those organizations that:

--   seek and find unique media opportunities,
--   have an eye for the unusual,
--   offer the ability to defeat clutter and achieve breakthrough identity,
--   bring to the media planning and buying processes a sharply refined understanding of clients' marketing objectives.

Media organizations will become elevated to a position of equality with creative departments within the advertising hierarchy. The word "creative" itself will no longer be the exclusive domain of art and writing. Unbundled media organizations and media buying services will institute their own "creative" media units (heretofore called planning). Advertising messages will be designed to be synergistic with the medium of choice, and will be stylized to conform to the television programs and/or magazines in which they appear.

The media star is in its ascendancy. The ad industry would be well served by encouraging this process, since the viability of advertising as an industry depends upon creative, effective and efficient media execution.

❢

MEGATREND FIVE:

ACCENTUATING THE POSITIVE

Society has changed, but the media have not quite responded. Americans are dissatisfied with things as they are. Dirty politics may have worked in 1988, but not in 1992. President Bush's advisors did not listen; President Clinton did.

Americans want to see, hear and feel positive news and experiences. We have had our fill of tabloid news and yellow journalism. The perception within the media community that "negatives sell" is simply inaccurate. While ratings for tabloid-style newscasts may appear to win the news daypart, the combined ratings of all early and late news have declined significantly during the past ten years.

Advertisers will no longer associate themselves with tabloid journalism as consumers become more disenfranchised from the content. Advertisers will increasingly disassociate themselves from negative programming.

With the election of President Clinton, a new spirit pervaded society. When faced with overwhelming societal and economic problems, the starting point for a turn-around must be a renewed commitment to national self-esteem, not just as it pertains to our image internationally, but to our self-image as well.

Presidents Reagan and Bush deserve credit for inspiring the nation and reinforcing our broad worldwide agenda as a role-model and defender of democracy. But we also understand that we are human beings first, and the politics of hate and polarization rekindled our innate compassion and feelings for others.

Tabloid programming and editorial, whether it be news or entertainment, serves only a small and shrinking segment of society. It serves the very segment that we must reach with a message of hope rather than a message of despair. Audiences are not simply "eyeballs." They are thinking, feeling people who respond viscerally to the input they are receiving. Major national brand advertisers will no longer support television programs, magazines or newspapers that reinforce our fears rather than our hopes, instill hate instead of understanding, and that are in conflict with our newly rediscovered positive spirit.

As we progress into the 1990s, advertisers will shift their media spending to those vehicles that support and inspire society, refusing to support negative influences. This will not be in response to boycotts and so-called public interest groups. Many of these groups represent and reflect the very negative, hate-filled thinking that voters have rejected.

For the remainder of the 1990s, a megatrend is the emphasis on the positive, uplifting, informative and spiritual aspects of society, without the far-right or far-left wing associations with which moral, social and ethical causes tend to be affiliated. These are simply human issues, and advertisers will seek to be identified with and in programs and editorial that accentuate the positive.

MEGATREND SIX:

HOME SHOPPING

Electronic interactivity, as it has been dreamed about, exists already. Consumers are shopping actively and daily via direct communications links to warehouses. It's called home shopping and it is a huge $3 billion business comprising both home shopping networks and television infomercials. This business is likely to double in the next three to five years, and quintuple by early in the next century. Computer advances are not essential. New technologies are not required; the television and the telephone are all that is needed. Enhancements and interconnections between these two communications devices are inevitable, but even if no more progress were made, home shopping would continue to grow.

Home shopping is beyond a phenomenon. It is not simply a trend. It is an economic enterprise that will soon expand worldwide, representing our conduit for delivering goods around the world, bypassing distribution and language barriers and competitive restrictions. Taxation and duties notwithstanding, home shopping networks and infomercials can be instantly communicated anywhere in the world. They are the incentive for a single currency worldwide. They are the embodiment of our capitalism.

If Ted Turner globalized the news, Barry Diller (who has acquired an interest in QVC Network) will internationalize home shopping. Home shopping services in this country will continue to expand as manufacturers and consumers identify them as a viable distribution resource. Traditional marketers, who can no longer afford to compete for retail shelf space, will develop distribution channcls through home shopping via infomercials, shopping networks, or both. Established and new networks will develop home shopping services targeted to specific audience and merchandising segments.

In the future, the retailing industry will consist of stores emphasizing service, convenience or low cost. Home shopping offers all three.

Home shopping also puts media into direct competition with the retailing industry. Media will have the best of both worlds. Those brands that depend upon retail distribution will require significant advertising investments to establish and maintain high brand awareness and loyalty. Other brands will market themselves directly via electronic and print home shopping vehicles. The third category of products will be those brands developed and marketed by retailers themselves, and these retailers will invest heavily in advertising to increase consumer awareness and loyalty. Brand categories that will be marketed via home shopping include packaged goods, travel, financial services, computer hardware and software, home electronics, video and audio equipment and software, books, and media itself.

Home shopping offers a direct revenue generating opportunity that is too enticing for television and print media to ignore. There will invariably be fragmentation of home shopping channels and programs, followed by consolidation. Home shopping provides media with a third revenue stream to supplement subscriptions and advertising. It offers marketers a means for selling products at lower costs by reducing their distribution and marketing expenses.

MEGATREND SEVEN:

REGULATORY SEA CHANGE

While governmental involvement in business will ebb and flow throughout the 1990s, regulatory actions will have a major impact on the businesses of advertising and media. In the short term, it is apparent that the financial syndication rulings that restrict broadcast network ownership and distribution of programming will be discarded or dramatically diluted.

This change alone will have a major impact on the relationships between studios and networks. The aggressive thrust by Paramount and Warner into prime time syndication changes the relationship of these studios from network supplier to network competitor. When financial syndication restrictions disappear, broadcast networks will pursue new production/distribution relationships outside of the studio system. Advertisers will play a major role as a new landscape evolves, forging new approaches to program funding through direct involvement with studios, producers, network programming departments and independent organizations structured to facilitate these new relationships.

Advertisers will support innovative intermarriages that help lower production and advertising costs. International programming consortia will be supported. Creative scheduling initiatives that merge broadcast and cable airings will be encouraged. Networks will regain rights to program for portions of the prime access half-hour, opening up additional revenue opportunities.

The impact of cable reregulation on the television industry is having a major impact on both the cable and broadcast businesses.

During 1993 and 1994, the Federal Communications Commission, with the direction of Congress, will formulate its interpretations and rulings related to the *Cable Television Consumer Protection and Competition Act of 1992.*

The most important components of this bill are "must carry" and "retransmission consent." Must carry provides a guarantee to broadcast stations that they will be carried in a prominent position in the line-up of local cable systems within their coverage area. Retransmission consent entitles broadcast stations to seek payments -- or other considerations -- from cable operators in return for carriage privileges. Individually, must carry and retransmission consent are considered by federal regulators to be fair and reasonable. Together, they place an unreasonable, and probably unconstitutional, burden on the cable industry.

One or both of these regulations are likely to be eliminated or significantly altered by the courts. At the very least, enforcement will be relaxed by the FCC. We expect that must carry regulations will be eliminated and retransmission consent confirmed.

The end result of the institution of retransmission consent will be to drive broadcast stations and cable system operators to develop closer ties and interrelated business relationships.

While this may not have a significant impact on cable or broadcast revenues in the short term, it will serve to strengthen their dependence upon each other. Federal regulators may have unwittingly created financial incentives for the television industry to act as a single competitive entity, rather than two opposing forces. Federal regulators will increasingly understand that efforts to increase competition must be balanced by support for the existing broadcast and cable business superstructure. Core businesses must be strong before ancillary businesses can succeed.

The most destructive governmental action on the horizon is increased taxation of advertising, which will be devastating to media companies. As an alternative, state legislatures should consider imposing taxes on direct marketing, couponing and other promotional services. The end result of taxation on advertising will inevitably be lost revenues and a weakened economic base.

MEGATREND EIGHT:

SMARTER SELLING

Can advertising and media survive if they are commodities, to be sold to the highest bidder? In an oversupplied market, costs are invariably bid down, not up.

Many salespeople in the advertising industry today -- whether they be agency account executives, media directors, or media sales executives -- have built their sales pitches around their costs in comparison to their most direct competition. This is not smart selling. Agency creative directors have succeeded by establishing that cost should not interfere with the creative process. This same creative concept will be integrated throughout the advertising process. Cost will become secondary to the media selection process, as media executives -- on both the buying and selling side -- emphasize their clients' marketing objectives and creative ways to communicate, with impact, to consumers.

Advertising's great strength is its ability to generate and maintain brand awareness and loyalty. Advertising agencies are the primary communicators of marketers' brand messages to the consuming public.

The current wave of advertising agency reviews is a reaction to the lack of a clear vision among both marketers and agencies about the role and value of advertising as a marketing tool. Constant agency evaluations and reviews are as disruptive to marketers as they are to their agencies. The industry will be stabilized when media companies and advertising agencies focus their energies on the issues of brand loyalty. Trade associations such as the ANA,

4A's, MPA, NTA, TVB, NAA, CAB and RAB should cooperate to assure that marketers get the point -- that advertising is the foundation of their marketing plans and a necessary tool to establish and retain consumer brand loyalty. Tax codes should support the corporate commitment to brand building by approving brand equity as a valued corporate asset.

The advertising industry must come together as one to take on the direct marketing and promotional giants. Although it may be a David vs. Goliath battle, the rock of "brand loyalty" is a solid rock indeed, and one that most major marketers will accept.

Smarter selling represents a shift away from further commoditization of media. It reflects a coordinated commitment by advertising agencies, media services and media companies to rebuilding perceived value, developing enhanced environments for advertising messages, and providing better knowledge about audience response. Media companies will become rededicated to building their audiences and audience loyalties. Research will be developed to measure brand loyalty, and will become the essential core element for the renewed growth of the advertising business.

Although marketers will continue to seek the lowest cost vendors and media buyers will seek to maintain the downward media cost spiral, there will be simultaneous support for those creative efforts that enhance media value and deliver results.

Please use this page to order additional copies of

ADBASHING

or any of the following publications.

ADBASHING:
- ☐ 1-12 copies $17.95 each   ☐ Educational Rate $ 9.95 each
- ☐ 13-24 copies $15.95 each
- ☐ 25-49 copies $14.95 each
- ☐ 50+ copies $12.95 each

☐ Marketing and Media Influencers $45.00 annually
   (The quarterly newsletter of the Worldwide Marketing Leadership Panel)

☐ Media Accountability & Opportunities $295.00 annually
   (A monthly newsletter from Myers Reports)

☐ Jack Myers' Media Megatrends $3.95

QTY	TITLE	PRICE
	NJ residents/businesses must add 6% sales tax.	
	Shipping & Handling: Add $1.75 for first item, $.50 for each additional item.	
	TOTAL	

If tax exempt please include a signed tax exempt certificate.
International orders add 10% to total order.

I am enclosing $_____.   Make checks payable to American Media Council.

☐ Bill my company (Purchase Order only)

☐ Charge my credit card   ☐ Mastercard   ☐ Visa   Account # _____

Signature _____ Exp. Date_____

Send To: Myers Reports   Or Call: 1-800-642-4242
          322 Route 46 West   Fax: 1-201-882-5476
          Parsippany, NJ 07054

BILL TO:

Name _____

Title _____ Organization _____

Address _____

City _____ State _____ Zip _____

Phone _____

SHIP TO: (if different than Bill To:)

Name _____

Title _____ Organization _____

Address _____

City _____ State _____ Zip _____

Phone _____

(Attach a separate sheet for shipping instructions for multiple gift orders. Add $1.75 for each individual shipping order.)

Please use this page to order additional copies of

ADBASHING

or any of the following publications.

ADBASHING:
- ☐ 1-12 copies $17.95 each
- ☐ 13-24 copies $15.95 each
- ☐ 25-49 copies $14.95 each
- ☐ 50+ copies $12.95 each

☐ Educational Rate $ 9.95 each

☐ Marketing and Media Influencers $45.00 annually
(The quarterly newsletter of the Worldwide Marketing Leadership Panel)

☐ Media Accountability & Opportunities $295.00 annually
(A monthly newsletter from Myers Reports)

☐ Jack Myers' Media Megatrends $3.95

QTY	TITLE	PRICE
	NJ residents/businesses must add 6% sales tax.	
	Shipping & Handling: Add $1.75 for first item, $.50 for each additional item.	
	TOTAL	

If tax exempt please include a signed tax exempt certificate.
International orders add 10% to total order.

I am enclosing $_____.   Make checks payable to American Media Council.

☐ Bill my company (Purchase Order only)

☐ Charge my credit card   ☐ Mastercard ☐ Visa   Account # _____

Signature _____ Exp. Date_____   _____

Send To: Myers Reports   Or Call: 1-800-642-4242
         322 Route 46 West   Fax: 1-201-882-5476
         Parsippany, NJ 07054

BILL TO:

Name _____

Title _____ Organization _____

Address _____

City _____ State _____ Zip _____

Phone _____

SHIP TO: (if different than Bill To:)

Name _____

Title _____ Organization _____

Address _____

City _____ State _____ Zip _____

Phone _____

(Attach a separate sheet for shipping instructions for multiple gift orders. Add $1.75 for each individual shipping order.)